GET PSYCHIC!

ALSO BY STACEY WOLF

★

Secrets of the Signs

DISCOVER YOUR HIDDEN POWERS

Get Psychic!

STACEY WOLF

WARNER BOOKS

A TIME WARNER COMPANY

Copyright © 2001 by Stacey Wolf
All rights reserved.

Warner Books, Inc.,
1271 Avenue of the Americas, New York, NY 10020

Visit our Web site at www.twbookmark.com.
For information on Time Warner Trade
Publishing's online publishing program,
visit www.ipublish.com.

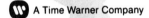 A Time Warner Company

Printed in the United States of America

First Printing: August 2001

10 9 8 7 6 5 4 3 2 1

Library of Congress Cataloging-in-Publication Data

Wolf, Stacey.
   Get psychic! : discover your hidden powers / Stacey Wolf.
     p. cm.
   ISBN 0-446-67797-3
   1. Parapsychology. 2. Psychic ability. 3. Psychic ability — Problems,
exercises, etc. [1. Parapsychology. 2 Psychic ability.] I. Title.

BF1031 .W755 2001
133 — dc21   2001017542

Book design by Jo Anne Metsch

Contents

Finding your intuitive light switch is easy. Flex your inner psychic muscles. Developing your psychic powers makes you more connected to who you are. It's time to get psychic!

Everything you need to know about the sixth sense — what it is, how it happens, and where it comes from. Take the psychic pop quiz, then add up your score to find out what types of psychic skills you have. Learn to identify your own psychic experiences and fine-tune your inner senses to have intuitive moments whenever you want.

Everyone is born with intuition; you just need to turn up the volume on your sixth sense. Find out what will happen at Friday night's party, discover what's going on between you and your special someone, know what he or she thinks of you — your psychic ability can even help you take tests!

Once you know how to tune in to psychic energy, show a friend. When two people get together, there is more psychic energy to play with. You can learn how to telepathically send and receive thoughts, use your abilities to read for others, and discover your psychic accuracy rate. Take the test and see which one of you has the highest score.

Groups have a ton of psychic power. Call some friends, focus on your inner senses, and otherworldly things will happen! This chapter includes ways to harness the intuitive energy of the full moon, have an angel séance, play chocolate guessing games—you'll even learn the technique used by the CIA's psychic spies: remote viewing!

Everyone sees signs. Some people blow them off as simple coincidences, but we know different. Signs and symbols appear in our everyday lives to tell us things and show us the way. This list is the easiest way to get the message. Learn the meaning of chills and shivers, flashing lights, different colors, flickering candle flames, animals, numbers, and more! The next time you see a psychic image, look it up right here.

Introduction

A_{LL} things psychic are popping up everywhere these days—in hit movies, best-selling books, and prime-time television shows. It's fascinating to watch the fantasy versions on the big and small screens, but can we get our psychic ability to work in the real world? The answer is yes—and it's easier than you think. Why? Because we're all natural born psychics.

That's right, you are psychic. The only difference between you and a psychic pro is that a professional can turn it on and off at will, and you haven't learned to do that yet. The only way your psychic ability has come out to play is through an occasional spontaneous intuitive flash—until you opened this book, that is.

The sixth sense is a subtle thing, and it can easily get drowned out by your other five senses if you're not aware of it. But your psychic ability is always there, even if you don't know it, picking up things as you go about your day—when you are talking with friends, playing with your dog, and shopping at the mall.

I know what you're thinking: If we all have it, how do I get it going? Finding your intuitive light switch is easy. You just have to learn how to flex your inner psychic muscles, something you may not have done before. In fact, you can even learn how much psychic potential you've been living with since day one. Start by taking the simple tests in this book and get an accuracy rate percentage for your intuitive abilities.

Old psychic books used to say that in order to develop your powers, you had to stand on your head and chant for half your life. Not anymore! Since we've hit the millennium, there is more psychic energy around than ever before. It's floating in the air, it's in our consciousness, just waiting for us to tap into it. This makes it much easier to develop your sixth sense with a little time and practice.

Not only that, but developing your intuition these days can be wildly entertaining. You can know how that special someone feels about you, send thoughts to your best friends—and have them instantly pick up their messages!

Developing your psychic powers makes you more connected to who you are; it helps you make the right decisions, and can impress your friends at parties. It's natural and it's easy. Discover all the great things your psychic ability can do for you—just turn the page and get psychic!

Basic Instinct

Psychic Class

PSYCHIC ABILITY 101

PSYCHIC ability, intuition, extrasensory perception, the sixth sense—they're all terms for the same skill. Intuition is a sixth sense that we are all born with, like our ability to see, hear, taste, smell, and feel. Psychic ability is those instincts heightened with an inner magnifying glass.

You've probably heard the official terms for these abilities: clairvoyance, clairaudience, and clairsentience. Clairvoyance is the ability to see images and pictures in your mind. Clairaudience means that you hear with an inner ear. And clairsentience is the term for people who pick up psychic impressions by feeling or knowing. Most people are psychic in this last way. They just *feel* something is right but don't know how or why.

Psychic ability has evolved since those words came into being. Now it's a blending of all the inner senses working together to give you instantaneous impressions. You can still be gifted in seeing, hearing, or feeling, but it's harder to tell where one ends and another begins. Basically, your *sixth sense* is a combination of your other five senses directed inward.

I did say *five* senses. Your other two senses come in psychic-speak as well. Believe it or not, you can have psychic taste and smell. You may have heard stories of people smelling flowers when none were in the room, or getting a whiff of their dead grandmother's perfume—it happens, just not as often as the other inner senses do.

There is one more inner ability to talk about, separate from the psychic abilities we've already discussed; that is telepathy. Telepathy is thought-communication, or sending and receiving thoughts and images with your mind. We all have built-in woofers and tweeters and we're constantly bombarded with psychic noise and information. It's just that we're not used to that kind of inner listening, so we block it out and pretend it doesn't exist.

In general, you are most telepathically connected to friends and family. The more time you spend with someone and the more emotionally connected you are with them, the stronger the psychic link. You can develop this link and make it work better, so that you can be connected to friends and family almost all the time. We'll get into some fun telepathy games in chapter 3, "The Buddy System."

Back to the sixth sense. We know that we have an inner guidance system—but what exactly are we receiving and where does it come from? Hold on to your hat, here's the answer: The world is made up of energy vibrating at different speeds; that is proven physics. Look around. Everything you see—the chair you are sitting in, the wall, the carpet, the television— is made up of energy slowed down to *look* solid. And it feels solid, too—anyone who has ever stubbed their toe knows this!

On top of that, this energy is intelligent. What makes the chair stay a chair? What makes the carpet continue on as a carpet? Why don't all the molecules just separate into one big mush? Because the universe has some kind of smart crazy glue that keeps everything in order. Psychic ability comes down to this: our ability to read that smart crazy glue with our mind; to rise above the everyday physical world to understand something unseen.

Now that we know where psychic energy comes from, how do psychics tap into the future to know things that haven't happened yet? That brings up more physics—Einstein's theory of relativity, to be exact. He proved that space and time aren't constant, that time moves more quickly or slowly in some cases than others, depending upon your perspective (where you sit in space).

According to him, time and space are very connected and very warped. So when we access that something unseen I mentioned before, that thing that bypasses our five senses, we connect to a time and a place where stuff hasn't happened yet. Whew. That is a big bite to swallow, but from where I sit as a psychic, it makes complete sense.

Now, how did we get from physics to psychics, and how can we develop these abilities anyway? Until we begin to develop our ability to tap into that subtle unseen force, we naturally have uncontrolled, spontaneous psychic experiences (everyone has had them, whether they are willing to admit it or not!). Think back over the past few months. Did you have a dream that ended up coming true? Did you have a feeling about someone that was correct? When the phone rings, do you know who is on the other end? Ah hah! So you know what I'm talking about when I say that unexplained occurrences happen all the time.

The more attention you pay to these spontaneous experiences, the more they happen, but you can take your psychic ability a step further. Instead of waiting for an odd coincidence to happen in your life, you can make it happen when you want it to by learning how to hear, see, and feel that unseen force.

Later in this chapter you will learn how to tune in to this energy and have psychic experiences on demand. Before you begin, take the psychic pop quiz and see how much psychic energy you were born with. Good luck!

PSYCHIC POP QUIZ

BEFORE you fine-tune your sixth sense, figure out how much natural psychic ability you have. If you're like most people, you don't like to take tests, but this one is different; it's easy and fun. Besides, no one can fail the test, so you have nothing to lose. Some people may be more intuitive than others, but everyone has some inner awareness—and this test will point the way.

When you are finished taking the quiz, add up your score and see if you are very psychically gifted, intuitively inclined, or need to open up your potential. You will learn how easy it will be to use your inner senses. You'll also get an idea of what kind of return you'll see for your psychic efforts. In addition, your score will reveal if you are naturally clairvoyant, clairaudient, clairsentient, or telepathic.

Get out your notebook and go for it! Circle one answer.

1) When you are talking to friends, how often do you know what they are going to say before they say it?

often   sometimes   rarely   never

2) Have you ever felt like you understood what a family member or a pet wanted with just one glance?

often   sometimes   rarely   never

3) When your sweetheart is away on vacation, how often do you know what he is doing?

often   sometimes   rarely   never

4) Do you actually *hear* a friend or family member's voice in your head when you are not with them?

often   sometimes   rarely   never

5) Do you ever hear noises you can't easily explain?

often   sometimes   rarely   never

6) When you are drifting off to sleep, have you ever heard people talking when no one is around?

often   sometimes   rarely   never

7) Have you ever been scared or nervous about something and heard a comforting voice out of nowhere?

often   sometimes   rarely   never

8) When you close your eyes, do you see actual images in your mind's eye?

often   sometimes   rarely   never

9) As you go about your day, do you ever see fast-moving flashes of light out of the corners of your eyes?

often   sometimes   rarely   never

10) When you daydream, do you see clear pictures?

often   sometimes   rarely   never

11) When you are drifting off to sleep, do unexplained images pop into your head?

often   sometimes   rarely   never

12) When you are in the middle of class or work, how often do you have a hunch and it ends up correct?

often   sometimes   rarely   never

13) When you are planning a date, do you ever get the feeling that something will happen while you are on it, and you end up being correct?

often   sometimes   rarely   never

14) When you are alone, how often do you sense there is something else going on in the room with you?

often   sometimes   rarely   never

15) Have you ever had a foreboding feeling about someone or something that later actually happened?

often   sometimes   rarely   never

16) How often do you remember the details of your dreams?

often   sometimes   rarely   never

17) How often do you act on your intuitive feelings or impressions?

often   sometimes   rarely   never

18) Do you easily experience a deep and peaceful feeling of being connected to animals and nature?

often   sometimes   rarely   never

19) Do you have the ability to concentrate for long periods of time?

often   sometimes   rarely   never

20) How likely are you to dismiss your unexplained impressions?

often   sometimes   rarely   never

Scoring the Pop Quiz: Part I

FIRST, translate your answers into the numbers listed below. Once you have figured out your total score, read about it in the following categories.

No matter how psychically gifted you are (or are not), your natural abilities will fall into the three different psychic senses we discussed earlier. Read the "Your Score Part II" section on page 14 to find out if you are telepathic, clairaudient, clairvoyant, or clairsentient.

Here's how to turn these answers into a score:

Often = 4 points
Sometimes = 3 points
Rarely = 2 points
Never = 1 point

20–34 Points: You'll Have to Work at It

EVEN though we all have a sixth sense, you may need a little TLC to get it up and running. You are not as naturally open to the psychic stuff happening around you as others. You could be processing just as much psychic information as anyone else and simply not be aware of it. People who think more logically some-times have a problem making sense of psychic impressions, so they deny that they even happen.

Also keep in mind that a lot of people fear the unknown. You could be shutting off your inner senses because you are uncomfortable with the idea of anything unexplained. To fix this, create more room for your intuition to grow, and learn to go with the inner flow.

Here are some tips: Be mindful of your sixth sense as you move through your day. Don't dismiss your impressions as nothing, don't judge your hunches, and definitely don't try to rationalize them away—just accept them. You'll be surprised at how your psychic ability will begin to show itself when you give it space to play.

35–49 Points: You Are Open to Your Potential

Y O U have good but mostly undeveloped potential. You probably have had a few spontaneous psy-experiences that you can recount in great detail, but you haven't gotten to the point where they happen on a regular basis. With a little effort, you can bring these inner abilities to their fullest potential.

Here's how to be psychic as fast as you can: When you play the games and take the tests in this book, make sure you take extra time to get deep into your psychic state. While some people are able to get information with light concentration, you may need to concentrate deeper to get the same stuff.

It's also very important to trust the information that comes through. Don't be worried about being wrong or missing the mark. Don't judge your progress against others, just yourself. Some of your friends may have an easier time opening up because they already use their intuition in their daily activities. Do the solo exercises and you'll catch up in no time.

50–64 Points: You Have Good Natural Abilities

YOU are used to relying on your inner feelings and instincts on a daily basis. You may not realize it, but you use clairsentient abilities to make decisions and often act based on those decisions. The difference between you and the super psychics in the following group is that your experiences are more unconscious than theirs. Because of that, you have a tendency to blow off certain psychic experiences by coming up with rational explanations for them. By not recognizing pure intuition at work, your abilities may remain undisciplined.

Your instincts can be trained, and it should be easy for you to make the most of them. When you experience psychic impressions throughout the day, it is important to take a second look at them. Make the whole experience of having an impression and acting on it more of a conscious process. When you are completing everyday tasks, make an effort to use your sixth sense as part of the process. Soon you'll be able to recognize your psychic skills and use them to the best of your abilities.

65–80 Points: You Are Super Psychic

YOU are the most naturally gifted psychic in the bunch—although you knew that already. You've probably always noticed odd coincidences and unexplained phenomena happening to you, and it's very likely that other members of your family are the same way. You are aware of these experiences as they happen and you even have some explanations for why and how they occur. The bottom line: You must have some good stories to tell!

The key to your psychic success is to control these experiences; to learn to fine-tune them, to receive practical information that will help you in your life. It's great to have dreams of dear Aunt Martha, but when you learn to fully operate your sixth sense you'll discover who likes you and who doesn't, know the best way to deal with your parents and teachers. With some practice you'll be psychically unstoppable.

Your Score Part II: Discovering Your Psy-Q

NOW that you know how much natural psychic ability you operate with, you can determine the nature of those gifts. Do you have good telepathic abilities? Are you more clairaudient, clairvoyant, or clairsentient? Do you have good psychic habits?

This section pinpoints your intuitive strengths and weaknesses. You may have had a low score and still have strong abilities in one area, or you may have had a great score and be lacking one inner sense. After seeing how you measure up, you may decide to pay more attention to the ability that is the easiest for you, or you may wish to work on the missing link. It's up to you.

It's important to know your natural psychic talents as you develop your intuition. Then you will know exactly what to concentrate on as you read yourself and others to get the most accurate information. Understanding your abilities will also help you to define yourself as a psychic, and will make it easier for you to talk about it with your friends.

The 20 questions of the test you just took are divided into five subgroupings:

> Questions 1–4 determine your telepathic abilities.
>
> Questions 4–7 determine your clairaudient nature (question 4 is both telepathic and clairaudient!).
>
> Questions 8–11 determine your clairvoyant vision.
>
> Questions 12–15 determine your clairsentient feelings.
>
> Questions 16–20 show your overall psy-Q, or psychic intelligence.

The first four groups that probe specific abilities each have four questions; the overall psy-Q group has five. Separate your answers into the different sub-groups and add up your score for each one. If you have combinations of three points ("sometimes") and four points ("often") as answers to questions in any of these groups, then you have that specific psychic talent.

The groups in which you have one point ("never") and two points ("rarely") are your psychic senses that need some work. If you have perfect fours in any of these categories then you are surely using that ability in your life right now—whether you know it or not!

Before you go on, review your answers to the pop quiz. Divide them into the first four subgroups listed above, add them up, and see what category they fit into.

4–6 points: Little or no natural ability when it comes to this sense.

7–9 points: Working, but mostly on an unconscious level.

10–12 points: Good but undeveloped skills of this sense.

13–16 points: You use this sense easily and effortlessly.

The psychic intelligence part of the test reads a little differently. These questions tell you if you have good psychic habits. If you already trust and act on your hunches, have good concentration, and a connection to animals, it will be a lot easier for you to use these skills to develop your psychic ability, no matter how you scored on the first four sets of questions.

To score your natural psy-Q, the fifth subgroup, add up your points:

> 5–10 points: To develop your psychic senses, you are first going to need to develop more inner awareness, discipline, and concentration.
>
> 11–15 points: Developing your sixth sense may seem unnatural to you. When it comes to inner guidance, force yourself to open up and look again.
>
> 16–20 points: You have the natural skills to develop good inner abilities. It should be easy for you to make room in your life for intuition.
>
> 21–25 points: Your mind works in psychic ways. No doubt about it, you are primed for six senses, not just five.

Not everyone has the same abilities, so don't think you are more or less intuitively gifted after reading the different scores in this section. Not all psychic senses are created equal. Just as some of us need to wear glasses, sometimes we can't do anything about a weak ability, and yet we still manage just fine. As you develop your inner senses, some will flow easier than others, and that is the beauty of it. Everyone is different. The key is to figure out how you receive information best and to work with your natural tendencies.

If you find yourself lacking in one area, don't worry about it, it isn't going to stop you from becoming great at this. I've been a professional psychic for ten years and, like most people, I have a weak link. Mine is clairvoyance. I hear and feel things all the time, I know who is thinking about me and who I should call back even before I get their message, yet my ability to see crisp images only occurs occasionally. This doesn't stop me from being a great psychic, because my other abilities fill in the gap. When I am describing someone's soul mate or future job, I get the details by *feeling* them instead. I have learned to feel images.

When you know your good and bad psychic senses, you will operate more effectively. As you go through the rest of this chapter and have your first psychic adventure, keep this in mind and see how it feels.

PSYCHIC STARTERS: THINGS YOU NEED TO KNOW BEFORE YOU DIVE IN

NOW you're all ready to experience being psychic. But before we begin, let's address some common fears and beliefs people have about this sense and discuss what it is really like. First, some people expect that names, dates, and places will just appear in their heads without any thought at all. At the very least, they believe that psychics have all the answers instantly — you'll discover that real quick the first time someone finds out you are practicing to be psychic.

Normally, when your mind is focused on walking, talking, and living your life, it is not in psychic mode, so it's not likely that you are going to pick psychic news flashes out of thin air at a party. You are working with either your five outer senses or your inner senses, not both at the same time. That is why you have to sit down and do a session or play a game to get answers to psychic questions.

Psychic mode is simply a state of *concentrating inward*. You are not in a trance, you are not being possessed, levitating, or speaking in tongues, and you do not leave your body — despite what you see in the movies. You are using a natural, normal sense we are all born with. You'll feel the same as you always do, except that you are receiving information from your head rather than from, say, a newspaper.

The most common fear about being psychic is that when you use your sixth sense, you'll pick up information you don't want to know. If you're like most of us, you're more interested in finding out what will happen on your next date than uncovering future negative events. You can forget that right now. Believe me, it

takes enough energy to receive the psychic information that you are actively searching for. Most probably,
nothing is going to come out of left field and surprise
you while you are doing this.

You may be one of those people who think that
being psychic means you're going to be hit over the
head with a wild revelation and be changed forever. In
reality, using your sixth sense is a subtle thing. It
develops at your own pace, and you will sense only the
information you set out to receive. Basically, if you are
looking for something earth-shattering, you should
put this book down and go skydiving instead!

Beginners are both curious and afraid when they
think of using this inner ability for themselves.
Relax—fears are normal. Just as most of us are born
with a fear of heights, we have built-in lifesavers with
our intuition as well. We are all a bit fearful of the
unknown, and this hesitation allows us to go only as
far as we feel comfortable. You may be scared to do
this *before* you begin, but once you actually start and
see how normal it is, you'll feel more at peace and the
fears will go away.

Everyone has their own comfort zone when it
comes to the sixth sense. Maybe you can easily get
into a meditative state without a second thought, but
your best friend only likes testing her intuition with
other people around. This comfort zone increases as
you play more games and take more tests. Before you

know it, you'll be doing all sorts of psychic things you never even dreamed of—no matter what level you start at.

TOOLS OF THE TRADE

THERE are many psychic tools on the market today. People use tarot cards, angel boards, I ching coins, medicine cards—some people even use regular playing cards. After you have learned to use your intuition, you may want to check them out. I love using different psychic gadgets. I collect them—but this book isn't about that. First you have to learn to quiet your mind and listen to your sixth sense. After you do that, you can use any tool you want, but you don't need them in order to access your inner wisdom.

The only thing you need to play the games in this book is a notebook. Get a very special journal and always keep it with this book. It's very important that you write down your predictions and test scores so that you can watch your progress. So often, after we have a dream or a moment of psychic clarity, we talk ourselves out of it. "Oh, I didn't really know that was going to happen, it was just my imagination." If you write everything down, there it is in black and white— exactly as you first experienced it.

Date each session, game, and test you take. Each

week, review your notes to see how psychic you are; you'll be very impressed by what you see. You can even write the time, the place, and the friends you play with. You may find out that during certain times of the day you are more intuitively inclined, or that different friends bring out the psychic in you.

GETTING PSYCHED: DOING YOUR FIRST PSYCHIC SESSION

N OW we can move on to what really happens during a psychic game. Here it is in a nutshell: First, you set your goals, that is, figure out what you want to know. Then you quiet your mind, turn on your psychic faucet, pick up some cool information, end your session, and take notes. It's a simple process, and it's important that you don't separate the steps or it might not work right and you won't be able to count on the messages you receive.

The first time you do a psychic session, you may feel chills, see colors, or feel nothing at all. On the other hand, you may have an all-out intuitive burst and see images and receive some meaty information, especially if you already operate with your intuition. But it is more likely that you'll just experience a hazy feeling. You'll know something is happening, but you might not be able to put your finger on it.

Psychic ability is like any other skill; it takes some practice to do it right and feel comfortable with it. Everyone is different. So don't let your ideas of how it *should* be get in the way of your personal experience. Allow your sixth sense to develop in its own unique way. That means, whatever happens when you do the following exercise is right—go with the flow and see where it takes you.

Let's go over each step in more detail so you'll know exactly what you're doing when you get there.

Step One: Setting Goals

BEFORE you begin, set your goals for the session. You need to have something to focus on during your game. Even professional psychics do this as they focus their attention on different areas of their clients' lives. A normal goal would be something like wanting to know what that cute guy across the hall thinks of you, what is the best class for you to take next semester, or how your summer vacation will turn out.

If you open up without being focused, you'll end up receiving mixed messages or nothing at all—and then you'll just feel like you're not psychically in tune. The different games throughout the book touch on all the different areas of your life, so by the time you are finished with the last chapter, you'll have hit them all.

For this beginner's session, grab your notebook, pick one of the following goals, and write it at the top of a blank page.

> Show me what being psychic feels like.
> Show me the best way to experience my sixth sense.

The first time you do this, you really want to focus on the steps and see what it feels like to connect to your inner senses. After you have done this once, you can repeat it to get a better idea of how it all works. The second time you do it, instead of just experiencing being psychic, you can ask a question that you can receive an answer to. Here are some good questions for a follow-up session:

> What can I do to get into a psychic flow?
> How can I best develop my intuition?
> What do I need to know in order to read myself accurately?

Step Two: Quiet Your Mind

BEGIN your sessions by quieting your mind. Our other five senses are constantly receiving information from the outside world. This buzz easily overpowers our subtle inner voice, and that is why many people think they are not psychic—because they can't hear this voice for themselves.

To bring your awareness away from sight, sound, touch, and smell, do your psychic sessions in a quiet room, sitting comfortably, breathing deeply with your eyes closed. To help shut off the outer senses, focus your mind on the air as it goes in and out of your lungs.

If you are easily distracted by noises or light, take the time during this step to shut them out. As you concentrate on your breathing, cut off the distracting noise or light from your ears and eyes by visualizing scissors cutting the connection and feeling the distraction drifting far away from you. You can also visualize a wall surrounding you, keeping you from fixating on the sound and light.

The first few times you do this, you may want to give yourself three or four minutes of practice time, but when you are used to it, this step should take thirty seconds to a minute.

Step Three: Turning On Your Psychic Faucet

THE second part of the process is turning on the psychic faucet—activating your sixth sense. There are a few ways to do this. Still breathing from the previous step, focus your attention on your third eye, the area on your forehead between your eyes. As you begin to concentrate on this area, you may feel it getting hot; then you know this way works for you. This is the best method for people who are clairvoyant.

Another way you can tune in to your inner senses is to focus your mind on either the area directly in the center of the brain, at the base of the skull, or behind the ears. These are common places for people to hear or feel their intuition at work. Another way to tune in to psychic energy is to breathe it in through the pores of your skin. To do this, focus on the skin on your body and feel the energy being soaked in like a sponge. This may work best for people who are clairsentient.

The games throughout this book have many different ways to connect. These are just the basics. Do the beginner psychic session, which is next, and then try them all. That way, before you go on to play the games, you will already know which one works best for you.

Step Four: Picking Up Psychic Information

ONCE you have opened the psychic doorway, you are ready to concentrate on the goal or question you have written at the top of your page. To do that, you must first make your goals really clear and then leave silent space to pick up the energy or information.

When you are moving from step three, opening your psychic pathway, to receiving (step four), you are going to stay as relaxed as you can and keep breathing deeply (that was the point of step two!). Then bring your attention to the question or goal and repeat it in your head a few times as if there is someone at the other end of the pathway that you are thinking toward. For the ten or fifteen seconds that you do this, shut out all your other thoughts, or you'll be sending out mixed signals and your sixth sense won't know what to answer.

When you feel like you have stated your intentions clearly and have really focused on what you want to get out of this session, stop repeating and just listen. Soak up the information as if it is flowing from some gas pump in the sky right into your head.

When you do this, don't panic and think, "What if I'm not doing it right?" There are a lot of variables in intuition, so you really can't do it wrong. Making the connection feels different to different people, and receiving information happens differently as well. It also depends on which way you choose to receive the information: through your third eye, the middle of your head, behind your ears, or through your skin.

The first time you do this, just concentrate on

removing distracting thoughts from your head so that you can feel what it's all about. After you have stated your intentions, and you move into receiving mode, you'll feel chills or see colors. Certain parts of your body may get warm, and you might even hear buzzing in your head. If you feel any subtle changes as you go through this step, you can count the session as successful.

After you have done this once or twice, you can move on to receiving information and not just energy. Here's where you write down the messages you receive while you are in your session. This is the first part of the process where you get to open your eyes a bit, or at least to split your concentration between what is going on in your mind and getting it down on paper.

The most common way people receive is by listening and writing in stream of consciousness as if they are taking dictation — only you might not actually hear words, you may only feel them. If you receive in this way, you have to trust what you feel you should be writing down and just write. You can also talk into a tape recorder. This is how I receive information for my clients. Sometimes I understand the whole concept before I speak, but most of the time I just open up my mouth and have no idea of what's coming until it flows out.

Another way people receive is by seeing images. If

you are clairvoyant or have a photographic memory, this will probably happen to you. What you need to do in order to document the messages is to describe what you see in words or draw the images right into your notebook.

Still another group of people will have an instant understanding and pick up a whole bunch of information at once, as if they are hit in the head with a snowball full of facts. If you are one of these people, you have to get out of receiving mode momentarily and write it all down before you go back for the next snowball or you might miss something.

No matter how this step happens for you, the best advice is: Trust the message and don't think too much or you'll cut off the flow. Listen, then write first and think afterward.

Step Five: End Your Session and Write in Your Psychic Journal

AFTER you have experienced your psychic connection and you have gotten all the answers you are looking for, shut off the psychic faucet and end your session. Do this by bringing your awareness back to your body and your surroundings. You may want to wiggle your toes or stretch your fingers. Open your eyes and ears to the sights and sounds of the environment. You can even imagine scissors cutting off the psychic current flowing into your brain.

Since your first session is just to experience being psychic, you're not going to have anything to jot down during your session, but your thoughts and feelings are important. Take a moment and write down anything that happened, any feelings or thoughts you have about your first psychic session, and any disappointments, too.

This is a good way to gauge your growth. By having it on paper, you can see the whole process unfold and know how far you've come. By the time your journal is full, you'll be a great psychic.

The end of your session is also a good time to review the dictation and the images you've written down while you were in psychic mode. While you are in a session, you cannot think and write at the same time, so it's likely that none of the information will make sense to you until your logical mind rereads it when you are finished. That is when you really get impressed by what your sixth sense can do.

PLAY THE GAME: YOUR FIRST PSYCHIC ADVENTURE

ARE you ready? You know what it's all about, now it's time to do it! We've already discussed the steps, but to make it really easy, here's a step-by-step list so you can follow along.

Do this exercise a few times before you move on to the more specific games in chapter 2. That way you'll know you've got your psychic connection hooked up and you'll understand exactly what it feels like when you do it.

Cheat Sheet

Set your goals for the session. Take out your notebook, date a blank page, and write down a goal or a question such as those listed on page 24.

Quiet your mind. Sit in a quiet place with your eyes closed, focusing on your breathing for thirty seconds to one minute, or as long as you need.

Turn on your psychic faucet. Concentrate on the area between your eyes on your forehead until the area gets hot. For your second or third time, try focusing your mind on the area either directly in the center of the brain, at the base of the skull, or behind the ears, or soak up the energy through the pores of your skin.

Experience being psychic or pick up some cool information. Repeat your goal or question several times with your complete attention, then leave space for listening and receiving the energy or answers. Go with the flow and feel your psychic connection open and running. If you've asked a question, write down what you see, hear, and feel.

End your session and take notes. Wiggle your fingers and toes, open your eyes, and bring your awareness back to your surroundings. Cut off your psychic connection with imaginary scissors. Write about your experience and reread any notes you took during the session.

Psy-Tips

YOU'VE just finished your first psychic session. Maybe you had a completely different experience than you ever had before; maybe you felt nothing; or maybe it turned out exactly as you thought it would (if that's the case, you can skip this section!). Whether it was stellar or just average, you may have some questions about your experience. Here are the big things people wonder about when they've just finished their first session or game.

First they ask, "How do I know I didn't just make up the information?" When we receive messages, we all feel that we are making it up, and there is a good reason for this. When you receive information from your sixth sense, it does not feel the same way it does when you receive information from your five outer senses. You are not going to have some concrete physical thing to point to as the source of your information. Your psychic powers work by using what is already in your brain to help you understand the message.

In other words, your sixth sense takes everything you know, like letters on a keyboard, and rearranges what's there to get its point across. Because the tools are already in your head, the whole thing feels quite natural. If we were taught growing up how simple it is to access these abilities, we wouldn't wonder if we were getting it right. Since we are expecting something difficult and earth-shattering, we think, "I can't possibly have gotten this correctly, since it felt so natural and easy. I must be making it up."

This questioning goes away when you build up some trust in your abilities. After you've done this a few times, you become more comfortable with what it feels like. Then it is much easier to open up and go with the psychic flow. Not only will you trust your abilities, but you can see how accurate you've been, and that is a sure sign that you're hitting the bull's-eye.

Your first session or game can also *feel* weird. There are clear-cut differences between hearing, seeing, and feeling things with our outer senses; this is not so with our inner ones. You may perceive a smell inside your brain, instead of with your nose. You may feel an image instead of seeing it, or see words instead of hearing them.

My abilities work this way: I feel-see and feel-hear my impressions. I feel myself hearing something as opposed to actually hearing a voice. When I act as a go-between for people's angels, I feel the words in my ear. However it happens for you, it happens, so don't try to make your experience fit the classic definitions listed earlier.

Another common first-session afterthought: Nothing happened. We are so used to being bombarded with bright lights, loud sounds, tastes, smells, and different textures that we are desensitized to the gentle sixth sense. Believe me, something *is* happening, whether you are aware of it or not. It just may take a few sessions to get your inner awareness to the place where it is conscious of what's going on in your head. It's like those hearing tests we all had to take in elementary school—if you concentrate enough, you'll hear the beep.

People can sometimes be very hard on themselves during these first trips into the psychic kingdom. They expect that everything will just appear before their closed eyes—images, words, feelings. Sometimes it doesn't work that way. In every class I teach, there is always one person who is completely getting it, but still they only hear a few words or sentences. That's a great first-time experience, but because they think that angelic messages must be profound, volcanic, mystical, and spoken in Old English, they deny it even exists.

Information from a higher source will be plain, simple, practical, and about the most boring daily things—it's really about life and all its issues. Some people have a list of dos and don'ts, shoulds and shouldn'ts, when it comes to psychic ability. For example, the only way you are going to receive profound nonsensical, wordy language from another era is if you expect that you are only going to get things that sound oddly like the Bible. The big reason for this is that if you only leave one channel on your inner TV working, you are forcing the universal glue to communicate through it alone.

In other words: Preconceived ideas limit your intuition. If this sounds like you, expand your thoughts about how you think psychic power works and release your expectations right now. That will enable all of your inner senses to work at their highest capacity so that you can enjoy the rest of the games and tests.

On that note, you have graduated from psychic 101 and are ready to move on to all the games, tests, and tips in chapter 2. Have fun, and don't take anything too seriously. Remember everything you just learned and it'll be a breeze!

ARE YOU GETTING IT?

Before You Get Up in the Morning, Get Psychic and Find Out!

Just to make sure you've got it down cold, here's a quickie test to give yourself. Do a beginner psychic session first thing in the morning. Your goal: to gather up five interesting things that will happen to you during the day. *Who is going to call you out of the blue? Will you get an unexpected piece of mail? Is your best friend going to be wearing the same shirt as you?* You can also do this for the next day before you go to sleep.

Do this three times a week. After a few days, review your answers. Get a rate of accuracy by taking five to ten days of predictions, adding up the correct predictions, and dividing the total by the number of days you have included in this test. Multiply the right answers by 20. This will be your accuracy rate. If you are over 80 percent, you're already a great psychic.

Don't like your percentage of correct answers? Do this for another five to ten days and try again; I predict your accuracy rate will go up within a week or two.

Sole
Searcher

Psychic Games to
Build Your Own Powers

Now that you know what it feels like to use your psychic abilities, you can move on to the juicy stuff. This chapter is filled with fun ways to explore your intuition—games that you can play on your own, anywhere, at any time; great techniques that will activate your sixth sense and make you a master psychic in no time. No matter which ones you choose, you'll pick up loads of information on just about anything you want to know.

Intuition Television will help you see anything and everything like a play unfolding in front of you. Play *The Love Psychic* and get the lowdown on all of your romances. *Meeting Your Angels and Spirit Guides* gives you a firsthand look at your heavenly helpers, and *Angelic Inspirations* dishes out otherworldly advice and wisdom from above. And let's not forget to mention *Revealing Dreams,* for all those mornings you wake up with weird images in your mind that you can't wait to describe to all your friends.

Along with these games is a test for the next time you go to the movies, a list of psychic foods to eat, and instructions on how to make your own psychic testing cards—the same cards the pros are tested with. You can even use your abilities to show up at dinner wearing the same outfit as your best friend.

Sound like fun? You bet, but before we get into it, there are a couple of things we've got to talk about, namely *questions* and *answers*. The key to most of the games in this chapter is knowing how to ask the right questions to get the answers you are looking for and how to handle the whole question-asking thing. Let's get into that a bit more.

ASKING THE RIGHT QUESTIONS

AT this point in your development you should take a more active role in seeking out and interpreting all the data you receive as you play all the games. Learning how to ask the right questions and clarify missing details will enable you to get the whole picture right on target with the least amount of effort. This may sound like a lot, but it's easy once you know how.

The best questions to ask are the who-what-when-where-how variety. Avoiding questions that require yes or no answers will free your intuition to do its work. You may want to know the specific yeses and nos—and it's okay to ask them—but you'll need more knowledge in order to act in the best way.

Here's a good example. Let's say you fight with your mother all the time and you want to know more about why that happens. You can ask:

What do I need to know about my mother?
Why is this going on?

What are the dynamics at work in our relationship?

How and when is this going to get better?

What are the best actions I can take in this situation?

As you can see, there are a million ways to ask questions about this topic, but each one is going to give you
a different answer. You also may find that certain
questions are easier to answer than others, so asking a
few will cover all the bases.

You make the choice. You can keep it light by asking fun questions, or use more serious questions to get
to know yourself better. There are no wrong questions—whatever you ask is right for you.

You can sit all day and ask questions if you have the
time, but if you're busy, pick the most important two
or three and do the rest later. When you are asking
more than one question, make sure you leave enough
space in your notebook between the questions for the
answers.

Most people love asking questions, but some people
can be afraid of it. Don't ask a question you are not
ready to ask. It's okay to not want to know, and in that
case, it is always best to be honest with yourself about
it. If you are scared to know something, think about it
for a second. Are you scared that you are not going to
get what you want? Do you already know the answer

but are afraid to admit it? Or will you feel better asking the question later? The answers to these three questions will help you figure out what to do.

Who are you posing your questions to? Your psychic self, your angels, and spirit guides. Everything up there, or, as I like to call it, the Universe. The answers you receive from these sources will always be fun and empowering, never negative or fearful. If you get an answer that doesn't make sense or that tells you what to do in a negative way, it is probably your own fears talking to you instead of your true sixth sense.

If that is the case, don't listen to that message. Ask the question again, but before you begin a new session, take a few minutes to release your fears and expectations. Breathe deeply and tell yourself that whatever happens will be for your greatest good. It is also good to do this if you're playing a game after you've had a bad day. Don't begin your session until you feel a sense of peace and detachment from your fears. Then you'll know your information is coming from the right source.

Asking questions can be both enlightening and entertaining, and making sure you do it right will ensure that you can always count on the messages you receive and will always have the best outcome possible.

When you receive information from the games in this chapter, you'll either pick up random words and images that you'll piece together later, or you'll see a flow of images like a movie, or you'll hear (or feel) a stream of words and write them down.

After the session is over and you reread your notes, two things will happen. One, you'll be excited about the messages you got, and two, you'll want to know more. The remedy: a follow-up round of questions!

When you reread your notes, and you find out that that guy in your Spanish class does like you, you may want to know the best way to approach him, or if he will make the first move. Scrutinize your notes, and if you want to know why something will happen, or when, or where it will occur, schedule yourself some more play time and do the same game again (and again) for as long as it takes you to achieve your goals.

Don't worry if the answer to your question wasn't the one you were looking for, and don't accept that you cannot pick up a particular piece of information. There are many ways to ask the same thing, and to get the whole picture you very often have to go back for more—this is a normal part of being psychic.

Okay, now that we got the question business out of the way, you are ready to have some intuition fun. Pick any game and go for it!

INTUITION TV: THE TELEVISION SCREEN INSIDE YOUR HEAD

WATCHING Intuition Television is almost like watching regular television—except your eyes are closed and the screen is in your head. There is no remote control, but all you have to do to change the channel is *think*. This game works really well for people who are clairvoyant, but it might not do so great for someone who doesn't see clear images in their mind's eye. Try it a few times and see what happens. You may find that this game brings up some good psychic stuff, even if you aren't exactly aware of how it happens.

Rules of the Game

FIND a calm and quiet place to play this game. No radio, telephone, or bright lights. You also need a notebook or sketch pad and something to write with. This should take you about 10–20 minutes to play, depending upon how long you like to sit.

Before you begin, take a few minutes to think about what you want to know or what you want to watch on your inner television set. You may want to know what will happen between you and someone you just met;

or maybe you want to find out where to go for spring break or know the outcome of your midterm exams.

PLAY THE GAME: WATCHING INTUITION TELEVISION

Set your goal. On the top of a blank page in your notebook, write the date and then ask the question or topic you wish to know more about.

Quiet your mind. Close your eyes, take a few deep breaths, and envision a TV screen in your mind's eye. See it light up as you focus more and more on the question you want answered, then concentrate on the screen. It's important that you concentrate on asking your question, and it's just as important that you then leave empty space for the answers and images to come to you.

Experience psychic energy. As you concentrate, images, feelings, or words should pop onto the screen. This will happen immediately, but it may take some people longer to get into a deep state of concentration than others. Draw what you see, write down what you hear and feel.

If you are a feeling person instead of a seeing

person, you can feel the screen in your head with the same intensity, or feel yourself inside the screen as part of the drama. When you do it this way, you'll be describing events very much like you would if you had just seen something, then closed your eyes and recalled the images from the back of your mind.

If you don't see or feel a flow of moving images, just breathe in the energy you pick up from the television. You might only receive a few words or a single picture, but that can be enough to bring you a sense of peace, and it's likely that the next time you'll get even more info than that.

End your session. Shut off the TV in your head, wiggle your toes, and open your eyes. Jot down a few lines about what kind of experience you had playing this game.

Your Scorecard

WHEN you are finished watching and writing, take a few minutes to walk around the room and stretch, then reread your notes. You may be surprised when you see the otherworldly wisdom pop off the page. If you have made predictions about the future, highlight them so you can look back at your accuracy.

If you received no words and images but felt a sense of peace and inspiration, then the game was a success. When your mood changes as a result of a psychic session, it means you did receive the information on an unconscious level.

Psy-Tips

THE first time you do this is the hardest, because you don't know what to expect, but remember, if you picked up just one single word, then you played this game right. After a while that one image will turn into pages and pages of images and information.

If you did the game and nothing happened right away, don't open your eyes and blow it off. Using your inner senses is new to you and the energy is subtle. You may need to try a few more times before it clicks and you start seeing things. You also may have to push yourself a bit. Start by writing down what you *think* you see.

Play mind games with yourself. Try thinking, "Okay, I'm not seeing anything, but if I *was* watching TV in my head, this is what I'd see"—and write it down. Believe it or not, you might need to short-circuit your brain in order to get past your ego and into that other place.

And if you did see images on your TV screen, the question you're asking yourself right now is, "How do I know I didn't make it up?" As I said before, trusting yourself is one of the biggest obstacles you have to overcome. After you do this a few times, your information starts coming true, and you begin to act on it. Then you start believing in your psychic self.

On the other hand, you may not be the clairvoyant type. If you are better at hearing or feeling instead of seeing, Meeting Your Angels and Spirit Guides and Angelic Inspirations will be a lot easier for you. Every psychic has their own unique way of doing things. Try asking the same question using the other techniques in this chapter; you may find that another game works better for you.

PSYCHIC FOODS

Did you know that some foods can make you more psychic? Here's a list of foods that will put you in a psychic frame of mind:

★ Poppy seed bagels. The round shape signifies infinity; poppies are used to make opium. I'm not telling you to use drugs — but poppies can't hurt you!

★ Green tea. Caffeine helps you concentrate, and green tea gives you concentration without the jitters. Plus, the color green is healing.

★ Blueberries and purple grapes. Blue is a color that calms you, purple promotes intuition, and fruit is a good light snack to have before you tackle a psychic game.

★ Garlic. Some people believe it wards off evil spirits—it'll actually ward off all spirits, living and dead, if you eat too much! It's also great for cleansing the blood. The less stuff you have in your system that's not supposed to be there, the easier it'll be for you to develop your ability.

More Food Tips

★ It's best to have a small meal with balanced protein and complex carbs about one hour or more before you begin playing a psychic game.

★ Don't eat too much sugar right before a session; it can make your mind a bit sluggish. Save the cookies for later.

★ Don't take a psychic test after eating a big meal. All your energy is working to digest your food, and you might not have enough brain power to do the job right. An almost empty stomach is best for psychic tests and games.

★ Fish, eggs, and soy burgers are better than meat protein when you're in the psychic mood. Meats and cheeses can be too heavy and grounding, and you need as much lightness as possible to promote your sixth sense. That goes for fried foods, too.

INTRODUCING ANGELS AND SPIRIT GUIDES

WE'VE been hearing a lot about angels and spirit guides lately. They appear on magazine covers, and star in their own TV shows and movies. The truth about these otherworldly beings: We all have at least one angel and one spirit guide who have been looking out for us since the day we were born. They may look different, but they have similar jobs—to protect us, to support us through everyday issues, and to help us accomplish our destinies.

Angel energy feels different from spirit guide energy, just like it feels different when we talk to a friend who is outgoing and sarcastic rather than a friend who is introverted and compassionate. You may have an easier time connecting to one or the other, and you may find after doing this game a few times that they have different jobs in your life and you can talk to them for different reasons.

Most of us cannot see our angels and spirit guides with our eyes, but we can use our inner senses to connect with them; that way we can be more aware of them every day. Here's your chance to meet yours and even ask them a simple question. Read the instructions twice, since there are two endings to this game, depending upon how much experience you have. This game will take 10–20 minutes.

Rules of the Game

FIND a calm and quiet place. Sit on a chair in the center of the room or in the middle of a couch, leaving empty space on both sides of you. Put your notebook or sketch pad in your lap.

Begin by closing your eyes, taking a few deep breaths, and getting into a psychic state. When you are in a calm and focused place, ask your angels and spirit guides to join you.

Sitting beside you on your left is an angel and on your right is a spirit guide. Turn your head to the left. With your inner eyes, take a look at your angel and breathe in its energy. What do you see? What do you feel? When you are ready, draw what he or she looks like.

Now turn your attention to the right. With your inner senses, take a look at your spirit guide as you breathe in its energy. What do you see? What do you feel? When you are ready, draw a description of what he or she looks like.

If you are a first-timer, stop here. End the game by thanking them, opening your eyes, and having a good stretch.

If you've done this before, you can move on and ask them a simple question about themselves or their relationship to you. If you are doing this you should write one of these questions on a blank page in your notebook before you begin.

> How do I know you?
> What is your relationship to me?
> What do you want to tell me?

Continue to breathe deeply while you focus on the angel on your left. When you are ready, ask your angel the question. Let the unspoken words and energy stream into your inner ear, or through the center of your brain. Write down whatever you receive. Repeat the question with your spirit guide on the right.

Finish the game by thanking them, opening your eyes, and having a good stretch. Write in your journal how it felt to meet your angels.

PLAY THE GAME: MEETING YOUR ANGELS AND SPIRIT GUIDES

If you are repeating this exercise, write one of the above three questions in your notebook before you begin.

Quiet your mind. Close your eyes, take a few deep breaths, and get into a psychic state. When you are in a calm and focused place, ask your angels and spirit guides to join you.

Visualize an angel sitting on your left. Turn your head to the left. With your inner eyes, take a look at your angel and breathe in its energy. Use your clairaudient abilities and your clairsentient abilities to get a description as well. Draw what your angel (or angels) looks like.

Visualize a spirit guide on your right. Turn your attention to the right. With your inner senses, see, hear, and feel your spirit guide as you breathe in its energy. Draw what your guide (or guides) looks like.

Ask your angel a question. If you've done this game already and are moving on to a question, continue to breath deeply with your eyes closed. Focus on the angel on your left. Ask your angel the question. Let the unspoken words and energy stream into your inner ear; write down whatever you receive.

Ask your spirit guide the same question. Focus your attention to the right and ask your spirit guide the same question. Write down what you see, hear, or feel.

Finish the game. Thank them and send them on their way. Write down in your journal how it felt to meet your angels.

Your Scorecard

THERE are two ways to know if you played this game successfully. The first is to explore your feelings. Do you feel a strong sense of peace around you or a tingling on your skin? Did your guides and angels make you feel inspired? That is the residue of angel energy, and it stays with you for a few minutes. The more you do this game, the longer that energy will stick around.

The second way is to review your notes and drawings. Did you get a specific profile? Are there conflicting pieces of information? Even if you only got a few words and scattered images, do they make sense? Does this information seem familiar to you? Are you comfortable with what you got?

Meeting your angels and spirit guides is like getting to know your best friend: The more you are together, the more you know about them. Play this game again in a few days and you'll be sure to add even more stuff to what you've already got.

Psy-Tips

THE first time you connect to your angels and spirit guides, you may not trust the images you receive. That is normal. Just go with it. After you do it a few times you'll know that you are making the connection.

If you saw something unusual, don't automatically think it's wrong. When it comes to angels and spirit guides, anything is possible. In my ten years of doing this, I've seen it all—animals, leprechauns, fairies, dead famous people, aliens, past-life family members, angels that are three inches tall, spirit guides that are ten feet tall, as well as groups of both. If you were getting something that seems off-the-wall, believe it— anything is possible!

If you didn't sense any energy, it may help if you ask yourself some questions while in this psychic state. When you are concentrating on your angel, ask yourself, *Is this a man or a woman? How old is this angel? Is she tall or short? What is his name?* The answers to these questions will pop into your head right after you ask them, so be prepared to write down whatever you feel immediately after asking. It's just like multiple-choice tests—when you go with your first instinct, you're more accurate.

Now that you know what it's like to meet your

angels and spirit guides, you can open this connection during the day, whenever you want to. The next time you need assistance quickly, see your angel at your side and ask.

CAN ANGELS HAVE A BAD DAY? AND OTHER ANGELIC QUESTIONS

Do you ever wonder what your angels and spirit guides do when they're not helping you? Do you ever wonder if they've got some advice to give you that you haven't asked for? Here's your chance to find out the answers to these questions—along with anything else you want to know.

Now that you've met your heavenly helpers, you can receive the full benefit of your relationship with them. Most people know they have angels and guides, but they don't realize how easy it is to talk with them, get their advice, and learn more about what they are supposed to do every day. Luckily, you know different.

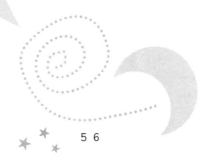

Rules of the Game

IN this game, you'll be connecting with your angels and guides and asking them a question or two about your life. If you have an area of your life that you would like to clarify, now's the time. You can ask your guides and angels as many questions as you wish. They will never think you've asked something too often or a question is too silly to answer. If you need help forming a question, reread the "Asking the Right Questions" section in the beginning of this chapter.

When you played the last game, Meeting Your Angels and Spirit Guides, if you had an easier time connecting to one or the other, you can simply pose your questions to that one, since that way you'll probably continue to have better communication. If you like talking to both, you can ask them both to answer, or you can tell them that whichever one prefers to answer the question is okay by you.

This game will take about 20 minutes.

PLAY THE GAME:
ANGELIC INSPIRATIONS

Set your goals. Write a question or two at the top of a blank page.

Quiet your mind. Sit in a quiet place with your notebook in your lap. Close your eyes, take a few deep breaths, and get into a psychic state.

Ask your angels and spirit guides to join you. You should begin to feel their presence within a few breaths.

Bring your attention to the first question on the list. Repeat it several times in your mind, telepathically communicating the question to them with your full awareness.

Leave quiet space for them to answer you. Let the unspoken words and energy stream into your inner ear, or into the center of your forehead, and write down whatever you receive as if you are taking dictation.

End the game. Thank them and send them on their way. Open your eyes, have a good stretch, and reread your notes.

Your Scorecard

IT'S very hard to put an accuracy rate to this type of game. In order to know if you've been successful, you have to go by your feelings. When you are finished talking to your angels and guides, you should feel excited and empowered. Your angels and guides help you by reminding you of who you are and what is important in your life. The more you trust their message, the more you'll believe in yourself.

When you reread your notes, ask yourself, "How do they make me feel?" If your answer is anything positive, you've made the connection.

However, if you reread your message and you find that it is fearful or the advice is negative, don't believe it. Ask again at a later time. Messages from above will always be loving and empowering, no matter how light or deep they are or what subject they are about.

If you have a friend playing these games with success, you can always ask them to talk to their angels and guides on your behalf. Friends are always great people to turn to for advice. Why not extend that to their heavenly helpers as well?

Psy-Tips

I T is not uncommon for someone doing this for the first time not to get it. It's like feeling around for a light switch in a dark room. You may fumble a bit, but once you find it, everything becomes crystal clear.

When I first started talking to my guides—or I should say, when they started talking to me—right before I'd go to sleep at night, I'd hear poems in many different styles of English. They were fascinating. One was so complex and used words in such a powerful way that I could never replicate it with my own writing style.

It took me a couple of months of writing down short phrases and poems before I could get real meaty advice and wisdom. Everyone is different. One of my clients went home after I taught him how to do this game and immediately began to transcribe an awesome amount of information. His life has been forever altered by an introduction to a world he never knew existed. If you are one of those people who starts out slow, don't worry, you'll get to the good stuff in time.

Everyone has angels and spirit guides, so it is pretty much guaranteed that when you open up in this way, someone or something will be on the other end of the connection to talk with you. If you're having problems at first, do it again. Try not to put too much pressure on yourself, and trust the messages that come through. The more you do this, the more they'll be able to help you.

HOME-ALONE PSYCHIC? TEST YOURSELF!

WHEN psychics are scientifically tested, a few methods are used. Here's one of them: A set of cards with symbols and geometric shapes are pulled at random in another room, and the psychic guesses what symbol is on each card. These cards are a great way to test your newly discovered powers, and the best part is that you can make your very own set.

First make the cards, then test yourself and find out your score and accuracy rate. The more you test yourself, the higher your score will be.

How to Make the Cards

GET heavy, brightly colored index cards and a pen or light marker. Pick a color that is the least likely to show through. Draw the following shapes on one side of each card:

Circle
Square

Rectangle
Triangle
Octagon (the shape of a stop sign)
An X

When you draw the shapes on the cards, don't press down too hard. You want to make absolutely sure that you cannot see any writing or depression from the marker on the back of the card.

Draw 30 cards, five of each shape; that way you can mix them up and safely guess 20 times without knowing what is left or having to stop and replace the cards.

Game Pieces

Before you begin, you need four things:

Your psychic testing cards
One large paper bag
One manila envelope that easily fits into the bag
Your notebook to keep track of your answers

The bag and envelope ensure that you won't see the image through the card as you guess and that you won't accidentally pull the card out face forward while you are playing.

Rules of the Game

F O R the best results, play this game in a quiet, well-lighted room and make sure there are no distractions.

THE TEST:
PSYCHIC TESTING CARDS

Make your cards. Place the cards and the envelope in the large paper bag.

Quiet your mind. Close your eyes, take a few deep breaths, and activate your psychic abilities.

Pull a card from the pile in the bag and put it inside the envelope. When the card is safely in the envelope, pull it out of the bag and concentrate on it for a moment. Use one of the following four methods to find out what image is on the card:

★ **Use your clairvoyant abilities.** Concentrate on seeing the image with your mind's eye.

★ **Use your clairaudient abilities.** Concentrate on your inner ear and hear what is on the card.

* **Use your clairsentient ability.** Focus on your feeling senses to *know* what is on the card.

* **Ask your angels and spirit guides.** Focus on your angels and ask them what is on the card.

Try each of these methods for 30 seconds. One or two of them will feel more natural than the others. If you are unsure which one to use, do each of them five times, and write down your guesses. The technique with the most correct guesses is the one you should use to get the highest accuracy rate.

Write down your answer. Pull the card out of the envelope and put it down next to you without looking at it. Keep track of the order of the cards by placing them in two rows of ten cards each.

Guess 15–20 times without breaking your concentration and end the test. After you are finished, go back through the cards and your responses and see how many were correct.

Your Scorecard

ADDING up your score is easy. Take the number of correct predictions and divide it by the number of total predictions. Multiply that number by 100. Here's an example: If you guessed the symbols on 15 cards and were correct 9 times, your accuracy rate is 60 percent.

You will test more consistently the more you do this. It's about getting better, not just scoring high. Play with the test cards for a week or two, then add up your total number of guesses and your correct guesses and find your average accuracy rate. The math works the same for larger numbers as well. An overall percentage that includes 100 guesses is going to be a better measure of your psychic skills than just 20 guesses.

Psy-Tips

AFTER you tried the four techniques listed in this game, I hope you had some luck with one or two. If you had a high score, great. If not, there is a little trick I sometimes use when I play psychic games. If I am not seeing something clearly, I think, "If I was about to open my eyes and look at what is on that card right now, what would I see?" You may be pretending to see it, but that just gives your unconscious psychic ability room to work.

Do this for a whole session and see if your accuracy rate gets any better. If not, you just may need to do it a few times to get your inner senses fine-tuned enough to get it. After a few tries, you'll tune in, turn it on, and your score will reflect it.

There is a simple, nonscientific way of playing with these cards that will still help you develop your abilities. Carry the cards with you throughout your day. At lunch or on a break, pull them out, facedown, and just guess what symbol is on the card on the top of the pile. You may not be able to get an accuracy rate this way, but you'll be sure to know when you are right and wrong.

If you become bored with the symbol cards, get creative. Instead of using geometric shapes, draw the following simple everyday objects: a house, a tree, a hand, a dog or cat, a car, the sun, etc. You can even use letters of the alphabet. When you get really good at this, take your cards to parties and test your friends.

HE LOVES ME,
HE LOVES ME NOT!

IT doesn't matter if you are single or attached—or have several irons on the fire—everyone wants to know about their love life. Whether you want to know what the new guy on the block thinks of you, what your boyfriend is getting you for Christmas, or who is the best match for you, you've come to the right place. There is no question that cannot be answered by The Love Psychic!

Game Pieces

THERE are some things you need to gather before you can play this game:

> A pink or white candle
>
> Pink, peach, or white rose petals (you can use another flower if you like)
>
> A picture of your sweetheart or something that reminds you of him
>
> A pendant or necklace, something with a bit of weight so it can easily swing
>
> Of course, a notebook

Pink and white candles give off a sweet vibration of love, and the rose petals help your intention to harmonize with nature. The picture will help you concentrate on the right person, and the pendant is a very cool tool to get easy yes or no answers.

Rules of the Game

FIRST you've got to figure out what you want to know. Do you want to know about one guy or a few? Do you have detailed questions? Queries with yes or no answers? Whatever it is, develop some good questions before you begin. Write separate lists for the yes or no questions and the more in-depth ones. Write them in your notebook, leaving some space for the answers.

In the beginning of this chapter there was a whole section on asking the right questions, but since questions are so important to this game, let's go over an example of two lists of good questions:

Yes or no questions:

> Does Dylan like me in a romantic way?
> Does Dylan like me enough to ask me out?
> Does Dylan like someone else?
> If I take the right actions, will I be able to get Dylan to be mine?

Advice questions:

> What does Dylan think of me?
> What actions can I take to get Dylan interested without turning him off?
> What are his favorite gifts and hobbies?
> If we do go out, what will our relationship be like?

The answers to the yes or no questions will give you a good idea of what to ask when you focus on your more detailed questions, so you can go through the first set before you write the second. Yeses and nos are also great for streamlining the session; you won't waste a lot of time getting right to the heart of the matter, that's for sure!

There is something going on here besides asking questions when you play this game. When we like someone, sometimes our wishes stop us from seeing the situation clearly. What you *want* to happen and what is *going* to happen are two different things. Since desires can hinder your psychic ability, you need to be able to put your wishes aside while you do this or you won't be able to rely on the information.

It's easy to do this. Take a minute to think, "Whatever happens is for the best, and for the next few minutes I want to connect to my higher wisdom and let go of my desires."

One thing before you play the game: When most people want to know about their love lives, they want to know everything. That's why this game has two types of questions—but it does make the whole thing really long. If you've done this before, or only have one or two quick questions, feel free to skip the steps that don't apply to the questions that you are asking.

PLAY THE GAME:
THE LOVE PSYCHIC

Set your goals. First you've got to figure out what you want to know.

Put the picture or remembrance in front of you. Light the candle, and have a small bowl of rose petals nearby.

Quiet your mind. Close your eyes, take a few deep breaths, and awaken your psychic senses. When you are calm and relaxed, bring your attention to the first yes or no question.

Hold the pendant between your thumb and forefinger. Make sure it's as still as possible. Focus your intuitive attention on the first question, repeat it a few times, and throw a few rose petals on or near the remembrance.

Watch the pendant move in a specific direction. Most of the time it will begin to swing slowly but very obviously in one direction or another even though you aren't moving your fingers — clockwise for yes or counterclockwise for no. Write down the answer in your notebook and move to the next question, repeating the process with the rose petals again. Do all of your yes or no questions this way.

Experience being psychic. Clear the petals away from your picture and concentrate on the image in your mind's eye, ask the first in-depth question, and start writing whatever pops into your head. When you are finished answering the question, your mind will suddenly feel disconnected from the words and images. Move on to the next question.

End your session by blowing out the candle. If you like the rose petals, leave them on the picture for a little while before you clean them up.

Your Scorecard

IT'S easy to score this test. Give your answers time and you'll see them come true right before your eyes — or not. If you picked up information that was really helpful, then you scored big-time, but any information that is right is great.

The feelings you get after playing this game are just as important as the factual, predictive stuff. As you reread your notes, do they feel right to you? Are you inspired or scared? Do they shed light on your situation or make you more confused? The answers to these questions will determine if you really connected or not.

If the information was insightful and makes you feel good about yourself and your love life, then you accomplished your goal. If the messages were fearful and made you feel like you have no options, then do some more inner research before believing them.

Even if you're good at this game, you can still get it wrong sometimes. Consider the ratio of one wrong prediction to every four correct ones to be very successful. Eventually you can get your wrong predictions down to one in eight or nine — then you can be the love psychic for everyone you know!

Psy-Tips

WHEN you ask many questions in one session, it's likely that you won't get awesome answers to every single one. If you don't receive a clear answer on one of the questions, you can skip it and still consider the game a success. You should get enough information from the other answers that one question won't make that much of a difference.

If you find yourself missing more than one, don't be too hard on yourself. This is normal for beginners, and you'll probably find that the number of unanswered questions gets smaller each time you do this game. Besides the beginner's theory, there are a few other reasons why you might stumble on a question, and a few things you can do about it.

It could be the wording of the query. Your psychic powers may have more to say, but the way the question is written there is not enough space to answer. You can take care of that by rewriting the question to give you a more in-depth answer and asking it with the next series of questions.

The other reason for a confused answer is that your desire to get a certain response is getting in the way of the process. Go back to the "Rules of the Game" section and reread how to get out of your own way—make sure you do that before your next session.

If you are having problems getting answers to the more detailed questions, try posing the question directly to the image in your mind, such as, "What do you think of me?" See, hear, or feel the picture talk back to you, and write down what you hear as if you are writing down a real conversation.

If you still don't get anything, try my favorite trick. Tell yourself, "I'm not really seeing or hearing anything, but if I *was*, what would I be seeing or hearing?" and write it down.

Before we go on, let's discuss accuracy for a minute. If you are reading this a few days after you played the game and things didn't turn out the way you thought they would, don't automatically think you got it wrong. When it comes to relationships, you've got two people's free will involved in an outcome, and things can change. You may have thought you got it right during your session, just to see things change course a few days later. Sometimes you can feel the path shifting, and that's a great time to go back to this game with a set of follow-up questions.

The more you do this, the easier it becomes to get more accurate and consistent answers. Don't give up if you missed some details the first time.

SIXTH SENSE: THE MOVIE TEST

I F you're like most people, you go to the movies and you watch TV. I bet you never knew that all this movie and TV watching is good for your psychic development. Whether you go to a movie, rent one, or watch your favorite TV show, you can use your inner abilities to determine what you are going to see before you see it.

A lot of these games and tests deal with knowing something before it happens. When you play, you can get all sorts of valid messages, but because you're not getting immediate feedback, you never know how accurate you are. This is a good test to determine how much correct information you can receive in advance about something that hasn't happened yet. Because you can watch the movie or TV show right after you finish your predictions about it, this test is instant truth.

As you've seen throughout this book, sometimes it's hard to put a concrete score on information you receive psychically. But not in this case. While you enjoy the movie, you can actually count the number of things you wrote that are correct and put an accuracy rate to your predictions.

This is a test of your precognitive skills, or your

ability to see future events. It doesn't matter whether you are using your inner sight, hearing, or feeling senses to do it. Once you are good at this, you can do it every time you need to know what is going to happen in the future—at a big party, a special date, or a final exam.

Rules of the Game

BEFORE you begin, you need to have a movie or TV show in mind. You can't do this without the exact movie title you are going to see or the show you are planning to watch. Your goal must be something concrete, like "The new *Star Trek* movie," not something like, "Later I'm renting an action flick." If you pick a TV series to play with, make sure it's not a rerun, so that there is no way you could've seen it already.

Chances are that you've seen a trailer for the movie, or a promo for the TV show, so this can't be a scientific test. But even if you know what the movie is about, there are plenty of descriptive tidbits of information you can pick up that you don't already know about; that's the stuff we're going to score at the end of this test.

Let's go over these a bit. You'll be good at seeing an inner movie if you easily see images in your mind's eye or have tested well for clairvoyance. Clairsentience, the feeling sense, is what the second way is all about. Feel yourself describing the scene by being right in the center of the action or even taking on one of the characters' actions. If you've had success asking your angels or spirit guides questions already, this is a good way for you to go. The last way is talking to the characters. Write down what they tell you as you have your pretend dialogue with them.

One more thing: Some people don't like to know anything about what they are making predictions about. If that is the case with you, you can pick a foreign film to test with or a TV show with an ambiguous title that is airing on an obscure cable network you've never seen before. Try this both ways, both with a movie you know a little about and one you know nothing about, and see which way you find easier.

THE TEST: INTUITION AT THE MOVIES

Pick a movie or TV show. Write the name of the movie and the actor starring in it at the top of a blank page in your notebook with the numbers 1 through 20 going down a column on the left of the paper.

Quiet your mind. Close your eyes, take a few deep breaths, and get into a psychic state. When you are in a relaxed and receptive frame of mind, bring your awareness to the movie.

Pick one of the four techniques:

* Focus your attention on your third eye and watch the movie on your inner screen.
* Feel yourself in the movie surrounded by dialogue and action.
* Ask your angels and spirit guides about the movie and write down the dialogue.
* Ask questions directly to the characters in the movie. See or hear them talking back to you.

You probably won't be good at every one of these methods, but do this a few times and you'll see a pattern with your inner senses. Whenever you need to get the lowdown on an upcoming event, you'll know which ones work best for you by taking this test.

Experience being psychic. Once you have chosen the technique, concentrate on the movie's general plot and action. Write down a sequence of events like a flow sheet running down the page, every plot twist getting its own number.

Choose another technique and focus on the characters. Concentrate on the first character and describe their personality, their talents, and the costumes they are wearing. Focus on what type of relationship the characters have with one another. Write down what happens between them and what props they use. Each prediction should have its own number.

Watch the movie. As your predictions come true, put a check mark near the number. When the movie is over, read the "Your Scorecard" section and review your notes.

Your Scorecard

YOUR predictions will fall into three categories. The first one is a direct hit, a specific and correct prediction. You wrote that the main character has a gun in his left boot and he does. The second category is near miss, a prediction that is close but misses the bull's-eye by a specific detail. Maybe you wrote that there was a scene in a car where the two characters have their first kiss, but the scene is in a bus or in a parking lot instead.

The third category is a complete miss, where something you write just doesn't come true at all. Review your notes, and give yourself two points for every direct hit and one point for every near miss prediction. Cross off the complete misses that didn't come true.

To get an accuracy rate for this game:

> Double the amount of total predictions you made to get the perfect score.
> Add up all of your direct hit and near miss points to get your score.
> Divide the perfect score by your score.
> Multiply that number by 100.

For example, Veronica made 25 predictions. Her perfect score is 50 points. She got 10 direct hits for 20 points and 10 near miss points for a score of 30. Fifty divided by 30 times 100 equals an accuracy of 60 percent.

Here's what the percentages mean:

> Under 50 percent = Bad test takers and first-time jitters. Play this game again.
> 50 percent–65 percent = You're getting it. You'll get better the more you do this.
> 66 percent–75 percent = Good. You're consistently getting psychic information.
> 76 percent–85 percent = Great. Be proud of this high percentage.

Above 86 percent = Terrific. Psychics don't need to reach 100 percent to get a perfect score. There's always a chance you're going to be off on one thing or another; that's perfectly okay!

Psy-Tips

DON'T worry if you didn't get it on the first or second try. Just like you may have had to do some of the games again in order to get into the flow, you might need some time to develop this skill as well. Once you find the on switch, it will be very easy for you to pick up information in this way.

There are two ways you can make your precognitive skills better. One, you can try the game four separate times, one time for each technique, and get an accuracy rate for each ability. That way you'll know which is the best one to work on. The second way is to try the game three to five times for practice, picking up information through each of the four techniques in the same session. After a few tries, I guarantee you'll get it.

PLAY PSYCHIC TWINS!

The next time you meet a friend at dinner or at a party, you can show up in the exact same outfit without planning it with her in advance! It's easy—and it's a good test of your new powers. Here's how to do it:

An hour or two before you are supposed to meet, take a few minutes to get into a psychic state. Visualize your friend standing in front of you; if you are a clairsentient person, you can feel her image in your mind's eye. Ask yourself a few questions. What is she wearing right now? How is her hair done? What shoes is she wearing? What kind of makeup does she have on?

It may come really easily. If not, keep your notebook handy and force yourself to write descriptions or draw images. Then show up at the party looking as close to the vision as possible. One look and you'll know if you got it right.

Note: Don't let your friend in on your little scheme—you don't want her changing at the last minute!

IN YOUR DREAMS, BABY!

W E all dream. Some dreams are full of random, wacky symbols, while others are like watching a movie. Whether they help us deal with unresolved issues, give us an opportunity to see our dead relatives, or contain predictions about the future, dreams are a great way for our sixth sense to communicate with us.

But no matter how great they are, there is a big drawback when it comes to dreams—they can be difficult to understand. When we sleep, our defenses are down and our logical mind is shut away; that enables the messages to come through. The hitch is that our brain works differently when the logical part of it is turned off, so with a dream, what you see isn't what you get. Symbols in sleep can actually mean something completely different to your conscious mind, and unless you are aware of how this process works, you can be confused about what it all means.

In this game, you'll learn how to play with your dreams, find out what they really mean, and get some enlightening information out of them as well. You begin before you begin, by keeping track of your dreams. You may be one of those people who wakes up in the morning and remembers everything. If not, start by keeping a dream diary. Let's face it, you can't interpret something you can't remember!

There are two ways to keep a dream diary. One is to have a notebook next to your bed. Before you go to sleep, tell yourself to wake up right after you've had a dream and write it down. A part of you will wake up and jot down the details, then in the morning it's all right there, even things you didn't remember.

If you don't want your sleep to be disturbed, tell yourself to remember your dreams in the morning when you wake up. Then, before you get out of bed, even before you fully open your eyes, grab the notebook and write them down.

If you are a really deep sleeper, it may take a few days of this before you wake up knowing your dreams, so give yourself a break and try it for a week. Once your brain is trained, you'll do it automatically.

You've probably dreamed a few dreams that have had such an impact on you that you remember them in vivid detail. You can start with one of those in this game, or better yet, you can use a dream you had recently. That way you'll be figuring out something that will have an immediate impact on your life today.

Before you dive into the game, let's talk about the different symbols in dreams for a minute and what they really mean. When you translate the symbol into everyday waking language, you have to listen carefully and release any expectations you may have had.

What you *think* it means and what it *really* means can be two different things. When you're talking dream interpretation, the reality can be quite different than it seems.

Let me give you some examples so you can see how crazy some of these symbols and their translations can be. If you dream of swords coming at you, that could be your friends who want something from you that you don't want to give them; or the swords could be obstacles in the way of your getting what you want; or they could be your dreams and goals if you are afraid of them.

On a radio show I was on once, a woman called and asked me about a dream. In her dream, she and her family were in a boat floating down some rapids and the boat fell apart. I asked her if they were thinking about selling her house, and she said yes. The boat was a house, and she was afraid that everything would fall apart if she moved. She was excited about moving, and didn't even realize she had some fears until that moment.

Now that you know how tricky symbols can be, pay extra attention as you go through this game. Have fun with it. You don't have to understand everything to get the whole picture. If you are having a hard time with one aspect of a dream, you can always go to the Dictionary of Psychic Signs and Symbols at the back of the book and use it to guide you.

Rules of the Game

Y O U can't work without a dream. Every game has a goal, and this game's goal is to dissect a dream. If you don't have a detailed dream that stands out in your mind, start a dream diary (reread the first section of this game). After a week of that, you'll have a few to choose from.

PLAY THE GAME: REVEALING DREAMS

Set your goals. Write a dream down on a new page in your psychic notebook. List all the details that you would like to know the meanings of and leave a space for the answer.

Quiet your mind. Sit in a quiet place with your notebook on your lap. Close your eyes, take a few deep breaths, and turn on your psychic flow.

Review your dream. Bring your attention to the dream you are playing with. Take a minute or two and relive the dream down to the smallest details.

Experience being psychic. Figure out what the dream means by repeating the following question to yourself: "What does this mean?" Leave space for the answer to flow to you.

Use your clairvoyant abilities. Bring your attention to the picture in your mind's eye for 30 seconds. Concentrate on seeing the image, and write it down or draw it in your notebook.

Use your clairaudient abilities. Concentrate on hearing the information with your inner ear for 30 seconds, and write down what you hear.

Use your clairsentient ability. Focus on your feeling senses for 30 seconds to *know* what the dream means. Ask yourself the question, "What do I *feel* this means?" and write down the answer.

Understand the individual symbols. Bring your attention to the first symbol on your list and think about it for a few seconds. Using the same three techniques, ask yourself, "What does this mean?" Write down the information you receive. Do this for the rest of the items on your list.

End your session with a good stretch and reread your notes. You may continue to have insights into your dream throughout the day, even after you have finished playing this game.

Your Scorecard

SOMETIMES it's very easy to find out if your dream interpretations are correct. If your dream was about a future event, you just have to wait and see. It's not so easy to know if you are right when it comes to problems in your life. Now that you know this information, you have to pay extra attention to what you feel and do throughout the day. If you are more aware of the problem, or feel that it might be resolved after this game, then you scored a direct hit.

If you played the game and got a message that you don't feel makes any sense, don't automatically think it is wrong. Opening up to your sixth sense can be difficult enough, so receiving any information is good—whether it makes sense or not. The better you get, the clearer it will become. But besides that, often our dreams deal with unconscious stuff, the fears and issues that we don't have access to during our waking hours. If your message doesn't make sense to you now, give it a couple of days and see if it makes sense then. You might just need some time to let it sink in.

Psy-Tips

REVEALING DREAMS is another game that can take a few tries. Everyone has their own way of receiving messages and their own vocabulary of symbols, and it may take your brain some time getting used to translating this new language. Don't take yourself too seriously as you do this and don't worry about what you're *not* picking up.

How much information you get will also depend on your comfort zone for knowing your unconscious stuff. Some people love to get to the bottom of things, while others are afraid things will come up that they don't want to know.

If you have some fears, don't worry. I can assure you, no matter how comfortable you are with dream interpretation, you will only pick up the messages you are supposed to pick up. Your intuition has a built-in buffer system that makes it nearly impossible to get stuff you can't completely understand or something that you are not supposed to know.

If you had a hard time receiving anything, or picked up fragmented information, try the game again, but before you do, relax and lighten up. Getting to know this part of you takes time. The more you do it, the better you'll become.

LOVE THE PHONE?
THEN THIS IS THE TEST FOR YOU!

The next time the phone rings, guess who is on the other end. Before you pick it up, make a split-second psychic judgment and blurt out a specific name. Do this for a week, keeping track of your predictions.

To get your accuracy rate, add up the number of correct predictions and the number of total predictions. Take the number of correct predictions and divide it by the number of total predictions. Multiply that number by 100. Here's an example. If Lisa guessed the caller of 80 calls and was correct 45 times, her accuracy rate is 56 percent. Do this every week and watch your accuracy rate rise and rise.

Here's how to freak people out: When you get it to about 80 percent, instead of saying hello when the phone rings, answer the phone with the person's name. They'll wonder how you knew that, and you'll be right eight out of ten times.

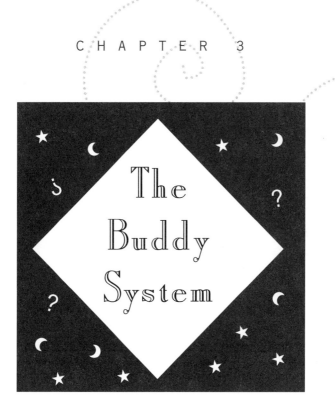

CHAPTER 3

The
Buddy
System

Psychic Games for You
and Your Best Friend

H ERE'S where you get to play games with friends, take some tests, and see how your abilities stack up against other people's. A big part of this chapter deals with something we touched on in chapter 1, an ability you can't develop on your own—telepathy.

Telepathy is sending out thoughts and picking them up with your inner receiver. We're all like telepathic sponges, soaking up thoughts constantly. You might not notice this ability, because we're taught to speak words out of our mouth and listen with our ears, so our inner systems are a bit rusty, but believe me, it's there.

Once in a while, we become aware of telepathic ability with people we know and care about. This is why you know when your best friend is thinking about you and why your mother knows when you've done something wrong. Telepathy is easy with friends and family because we have a natural link to them. It's not so easy with strangers, unless you are a very strong sender or receiver—and this is a good reason to practice. The next time you are at a party and spot a hottie from across the room, you'll be glad you did!

Along with telepathy games, this chapter includes fun psychic games, too, such as step-by-step instructions on how to make a personalized deck of guidance cards and give great psychic birthday readings with them. You'll also learn how to be a real live phone psychic. There's also a test that you can give each other to find out your accuracy rate. All you need is a deck of playing cards.

TELEPATHY PREP

BEFORE the first game, let's go over how telepathy happens, what it will feel like, and the common misconceptions about this natural talent. This will prepare you with all the information you need to do it and not get completely confused or overwhelmed your first time out.

Telepathy is sending and receiving thoughts with your mind. We do this all day long without even knowing it. We have so much buzz in our minds that we don't usually quiet down enough to hear it. When you sit down to play a telepathy game, you concentrate on this ability in your mind and shut out all the other stuff that usually masks it. That's how you pick up your information. It's always there, you're just listening to it better.

The first time you try sending and receiving, you'll probably have to concentrate a bit to pick up random details of the thoughts your friend is sending. Seeing a whole image in your mind's eye is nearly impossible for newbies, so don't shoot for that when you begin.

Just focus on your friend's thoughts and describe the images and symbols as they come up.

Believe it or not, you don't have to be a good clairvoyant type to do this successfully. You'll learn that there are many ways to send and receive thoughts and images. Whether you are a feeling, seeing, or hearing person, whether you receive in the center of your head, behind your ears, or nowhere specific, your efforts will pay off as soon as you figure out how you work best. Basically, no matter how you focus, you'll get the picture.

In reality, when you first play, you may feel like you're just guessing—that is, until you really know what it feels like. Take as many guesses as you can, because the proof will come afterward when you look at your accuracy. Like the rest of the games, this one gets much easier with time and practice. After you raise your telepathy comfort zone, it will feel like a natural knowing, an instant understanding of what is on your friend's mind.

People sometimes fear this ability. They think, "Are you going to know my deepest secrets?" The answer is no. Good telepathic abilities give you an idea of what is in the forefront of someone's mind—what they keep thinking about over and over again and what's got them very excited.

When someone has well-developed telepathic senses, they'll know when their best friend has something

important to tell them or when their pet wants something. Or they'll get a strong feeling to call their cousin
in another state. They are not going to know what you
ate for breakfast. Relax—your secrets are safe.

Using well-developed telepathy can also give you a
good idea when someone is lying to you or not telling
you the whole story, but you may not instantly be able
to get to the truth without a little psychic investigative
work. In that case, you may need to combine your
telepathic hunches with one of the games in chapter 2.
After asking your psychic self some choice questions,
you should be able to get to the bottom of anything.

Try *Sending and Receiving* with a friend a few times
and see how natural it feels to connect telepathically.
Doing it will put to rest any fears or misunderstand-
ings you may have. After a few tries, you'll figure out
how you receive the best, and the rest will be history!

TELEPATHY TENNIS, ANYONE?

YOU and your friend are going to swap pictures by
sending and receiving them in your mind. Playing this
game over and over will open up your telepathic abilities, so that you'll be able to receive instant messages
from your friends during the day without having to be
playing a psychic game. The next time something huge

happens to one of them, you'll pick up on it and be the first to know.

Once you get this game down pat, you'll find it much easier to communicate with a pet or a relative who is far away. One glance from Fido and you'll understand his needs. You'll just know when Aunt Mae is going to call and what she is going to say. You'll also be able to read people who you've just met or who you want to get to know better.

Game Pieces

T O play this game you need:

> Two 9-by-12 manila envelopes (or larger)
> Eight to ten magazines with lots of photos in them
> A parent, sibling, or friend to help you prepare

Before you begin, give one of your parents or other friends eight to ten magazines—the ones with unusual ads work best. Have them tear out the pictures and ads they find interesting, anything from cars to make-up to jewelry to cereal. They should have at least 20 pictures and make sure there are no duplicates. Mix up the ads, separate them into two piles, and put each pile in a big manila envelope.

Neither of you should know what images are in the envelopes before you begin sending and receiving.

Rules of the Game

BEFORE you begin, review the rules so you both know what's going to happen and how to play.

Sit face-to-face, across from each other at a table or about five feet apart on the floor. If you want a more scientific way of doing this, sit in separate rooms or back-to-back with a screen between you.

PLAY THE GAME: SENDING AND RECEIVING

Decide who will be the first sender and who will be the first receiver. Review the steps. Put the two large envelopes described above in front of you. Neither of you should know what images are in the envelopes. The sender should discreetly pull out their first image and keep it hidden from the receiver.

Quiet your mind. Both of you close your eyes, take a few deep breaths, and get into a relaxed, psychic state.

The sender acts first. The sender stares at the image and studies it in detail, actively sending thoughts about the picture to the receiver.

The receiver begins. With eyes closed, the receiver picks up all the information they can, describing what they see, hear, and feel. It doesn't matter what the receiver's best psychic skills are; you can pick any of the following techniques to get the image:

★ **Clairvoyance:** The image will appear in your mind's eye as you concentrate on the area on your forehead between your eyes.

★ **Clairaudience:** Concentrate on your inner ears and you'll hear descriptions or sounds that will tell you what the image is.

★ **Clairsentience:** Just thinking about the picture will bring up feelings and a deep knowing about what it is your friend is looking at.

The whole process should take three or four minutes.

Switch roles and do it again. Stop after you both have had a chance to send and receive, then share your pictures and see how accurate you both were—then do it again. You can do this back and forth until you're ready to stop!

Your Scorecard

YOU'RE not looking for an accuracy percentage with this game. First you want to get enough of an image in your mind so you know without a doubt that you are using your telepathic abilities. This may take a few tries. Guessing *anything* is a beginning, so don't worry about saying only things that are right. (Note to senders: Don't laugh, whatever they say; it may sound crazy, but it's all in the interpretation!) If you are a beginner, be happy if you get one out of three pictures correct or half the details of a particular image.

The next thing you want to see is improvement — how quickly you can pick up an accurate image, how many details you can report back. If you get four out of five facts correct, you've got it down. The more you practice, the more confident you will be in your abilities.

After you've done this a few times, you'll get the hang of it, and that is where the fun begins. Impress people at your next party or family gathering by having someone send you an image. You're sure to wow them with your telepathic magic.

Psy-Tips

PLAYING with your telepathic abilities for the first time can be just as nerve-racking as playing with your sixth sense for the first time. Until you know what a bull's-eye feels like, you may feel like you're taking shots in the dark. The good thing is that once you get it, you'll get it forever.

If you're having a hard time seeing or feeling the images automatically, try asking yourself a few questions about it. *Is this a picture of a person, place, or thing? What is the main color or colors in the image? What is the main action or activity in the photo?* You'll be surprised at how accurate these tidbits of information can be. You can also ask a third party to ask you questions—just make sure the person hasn't seen the image, either.

Here are some more tips to try: Pretend you are holding the image and look at it through your friend's eyes, and describe what you see or feel. Visualize the image right in front of you and touch it with your hands, then draw what it looks and feels like. Get inside the picture, putting your whole body in it, and describe what you see and feel around you.

Before you freak out, do this Sending and Receiving game five times. By the fifth time you'll see so much improvement that most of your fears and questions will be taken care of.

HIT THE DECK!

HERE'S a great test that you can take with a friend. All you need is a deck of regular playing cards. There are three versions of this test, depending on your level. If you've just started your psychic studies, begin with the newcomer game. When you feel ready, you can move on to the intermediate and extraordinary levels. Before you begin, pick one:

> **Newcomer:** Sense the color of the card in front of you, red or black.
>
> You have a 50 percent chance of being correct.
>
> **Intermediate:** Sense the suit of the card — diamond, heart, spade, or club.
>
> You have a 25 percent chance of a right answer.
>
> **Extraordinary:** Sense the number on the card — ace through ten.
>
> You have just a 10 percent chance of a correct guess.

Rules of the Game

GET a deck of playing cards and separate out the jokers and the court cards—that's all the people in the pack. You're going to be working with the 40 numbered suit cards. You'll also need a notebook and a pen.

Neither of you should look at the cards before you begin. The friend who is taking the test should never see a card during the test, even after they have guessed what is on it. Whether they are right or wrong, it may distract them from maintaining their psychic flow.

THE TEST: ACCURACY RATE EXAM

Determine who will take the test and who will give it. Whoever takes the test first is friend #1. Sit across from each other on the floor or a table with the 40 cards completely shuffled and placed facedown near the friend who's giving the test, friend #2.

Friend #1 picks the game. Newcomer, Intermediate, or Extraordinary.

Friend #2 takes the first action. Without looking at the cards, the test giver slides the top card from the pile and places it in front of the test taker.

Friend #1 quiets their mind and activates their psychic ability. Using one, two, or all three of the psychic techniques, pick up the card's image, then guess what it is:

* Clairvoyance: The card's image will appear in your mind's eye as you focus on the area on your forehead between your eyes.
* Clairaudience: Concentrate on your inner ears and you'll hear or hear/feel a voice or voices that will tell you what the card is.
* Clairsentience: Thinking about the card will bring up a deep sense of *knowing* about what is on it.

Friend #2 scores the guess. The test giver looks at the card, without showing it to friend #1, and writes down the guess, the actual card, and whether the answer is correct or not. Move on to the next card. Do this 20 times in a row.

Your Scorecard

TO find your psychic accuracy percentage, take the number of correct answers and multiply it by five. In math terms that looks like this:

number of correct responses times 5 = accuracy percentage

The way to find out your percentage is the same for each test, but the expectations are different because the tests have varying rates of chance. Look below to find out what your percentage means:

Newcomer Test (50 percent chance of accuracy):

50–60 percent	Could be psychic, could be lucky guesses.
61–70 percent	You're tapping into your potential.
71–80 percent	Your intuition's working well.
81–90 percent	You're really going with the psychic flow.
95 percent–	Off the charts!

Intermediate Test (25 percent chance of accuracy):

25–30 percent	Could be psychic, could be lucky guesses.
31–40 percent	You're tapping into your potential.
41–50 percent	Your intuition's working well.

51–60 percent	You're really going with the psychic flow.
61–70 percent	Very gifted indeed.
71–85 percent	Super supernatural.
86 percent–	Off the charts!

Extraordinary Test (10 percent chance of accuracy):

10–15 percent	Could be psychic, could be lucky guesses.
16–25 percent	You're tapping into your potential.
26–35 percent	Your intuition's working well.
36–45 percent	You're really going with the psychic flow.
46–55 percent	Very gifted indeed.
56–65 percent	Awesome talents.
66–75 percent	Super supernatural.
76 percent–	Off the charts!

What do these numbers mean? Realistically, you can't count on your psychic ability unless you consistently get scores much higher than the chance rate. For the Newcomer game that means over 70 percent, for the Intermediate game over 41 percent, and for the Extraordinary game 26 percent. The percentages get lower because the tests get more difficult. On the other hand, each test gives you a chance of scoring higher and getting much better.

If you take these tests several times, you'll begin to see a consistent accuracy rate. To find an average for your percentages, you can even take the scores of several testings, add them up, and divide them by the number of times you've taken the test. Share your results with friends and see who is the most accurate among you.

Psy-Tips

THE mantra of this book: Everyone's intuition works differently. And some people's intuition works in a way that is better for this test than others'. If you're lucky, an image of the card will pop into your head, but most people will have to work a bit to get the answer.

Try asking yourself a question: *Is it red or black? What color is it? What suit is it? What number is it?* If you enjoy talking to your angels, you can ask them for the answer. You can also put your hand on top of the card and feel the answer, concentrating on *What is the correct color, suit, or number of this card?*

When you are just beginning, maybe you will want to put aside the accuracy part of the test and just go with what you feel. That way you and your friend can help each other develop your abilities. If you do it this way, you're free to say things like, "I feel like it's red, but I don't know if it's a heart or a diamond," or, "I think it's a low number, two, three, or four, something like that." Your friend can be very supportive and say, "Yes, you're right, now try and guess further." Getting positive feedback can make you more at ease, then when you're ready you can take the test as it is written.

The more trials of this test you take, the more accurate you'll become. Don't worry about one individual score. Take the test a few times and you'll see your percentage increase each time as you develop your psychic powers.

The Perfect Psychic Birthday Gift!

WHAT is a good gift for a friend who is into all things paranormal? A reading with a set of their very own psychic guidance cards! In this game, you'll find out how to make a set of personalized cards and learn to read them with the very special birthday reading below. Your friend will love to know what's going to happen to them throughout the next year, and when you are finished, they get to keep the cards to play with, and you get a big thank-you!

Make the Cards

YOU will need brightly colored index cards, pretty shelf paper, and a few different light-colored markers. You can use one marker, but having a few different colors to choose from will make prettier pictures and words.

First you are going to write the cards especially for your friend. Here's what to do:

* Write out 12 cards, one for each month, and keep them in a separate pile.
* Write and draw 20–25 images of people, places, and things in her life: boyfriends, gal pals, teachers, family, pets, and things that are important to her like her hobbies, skills, and classes.
* Write out 20–30 description cards: things she says and words that describe the above people, places, and things. Also write out words that describe how these events can happen (for instance, "delays," "quick," "out of the blue," etc).
* Write or draw 10–20 events that are likely to happen to her and/or other people on the list. Stuff like: "romantic date," "vacation," "big exam," "work," "concert," and "party." Do not

write events that are on specific days of the calendar like Christmas and Valentine's Day.

★ Write out the 12 astrological Sun signs with the days they are active (for info on that, look up *Astrology* in the dictionary at the back of the book).

The numbers given are just a general guideline; the exact number of cards you make is up to you, but there should be at least 60 or there won't be much to read.

Once you have made the cards, cut the shelf paper to the size of the index cards and press them to the backs of the cards. This is to make sure that you can't see the images through the front of the cards. You may want to press the cards to the paper first, then cut around it.

Be careful not to leave any bubble marks on the back of the cards that will make one look a bit different from another. You don't want to be able to read them before you read them.

Rules of the Game

Now that you have the cards, you need to know how to read them. Let's go over all the details so that when you give your friend the reading, you know exactly what to do. Before you begin, make sure you have a notebook and a pen handy. While you read, tell your friend to take detailed notes.

After the cards are all laid out, take a minute to get into a psychic state. Close your eyes again and awaken whatever seeing, hearing, and/or feeling senses you like to use the best. Your friend can just sit and wait for the reading to begin.

When you are ready, pick up the cards for the month that begins right after her birthday. For example, if her birthday is in July, begin reading at August. Don't automatically start with January unless you are in December. You don't want the reading to begin so far in advance of her birthday that she has to wait to see what happens.

There are four things to look for when reading the guidance cards. First, determine the people, places, things, and events that will happen in that month, then connect the different descriptive words to them and figure out when during the month they are going to happen. The last thing to look for is cards that are right side up versus cards that are upside down. Some of this will be spelled out for you, and some of it you'll have to use your intuition to figure out.

The first few times you try to connect the dots, you may find it difficult to find a flow, but it gets easier with practice. By the time you're finished with the twelfth month, you'll definitely see an improvement in how you word things.

If you've got the wording down right and everything seems to flow, you can really let your intuition run free. Use each event and its description cards as starting points. Close your eyes and envision the event. Ask yourself, *What is going to happen at this event? What does she need to know about it? How is my friend going to feel while she is there?* Add these answers to the reading.

PLAY THE GAME: GIVE YOUR FRIEND A BIRTHDAY READING

Create a fun environment to do the reading. Have your favorite photo of the two of you close by. Light a candle and have some New Age music playing softly in the background.

Quiet your minds. Both of you should close your eyes and take a few deep breaths to relax. Give your friend the cards and tell her to mix them up for a few minutes. Keep the 12 month cards separate. Don't worry about the words or images being upside down when they're finished being mixed—you'll be able to read them anyway, and besides, having reversed cards is a big part of the reading.

Lay out the 12 month cards, then the reading cards. Line them up in a single row. Then take all of your mixed up reading cards and lay them facedown, one after another directly under the month cards, making twelve piles.

This is how it's going to look: Card #1 goes on January, card #2 goes on top of February, #3 is March, and so on through the first twelve. Card #13 will then go on top of January, #14 belongs on February, and #15 on March, up to card #24. It doesn't matter how many cards you have, just keep putting a card on each pile until you run out of cards. At the end, the first few months may have one more card than the other piles, but that's not going to affect the reading.

Quiet your mind and get into a psychic state. Close your eyes again and awaken whatever seeing, hearing, and/or feeling senses you like to use the best.

Pick up the cards for the month that begins right after her birthday. Fan the cards out or flip them over one by one so that they are in a tight little row of their own with the pictures facing up.

Look at the four different aspects of reading the cards. First, determine the people, places, and events that will happen in that month, then connect the different descriptive words to them and figure out when during the month they are going to happen. Before you begin to interpret them, examine the cards that are right side up versus cards that are upside down. Let's go over that step-by-step.

First, see what people and events come up. Keep in mind that the normal events that come up in that month anyway won't have a card, such as Halloween or New Year's Eve. You are also not going to have all the people, places, hobbies, and events show up in one month. There may be one, or four, but likely there will just be two or three, depending upon how many cards you have drawn.

Count up the different people, places, and events and use them as anchors for the rest of the reading. How close are the people to the activities? If they are separated by a few cards, then they are probably not connected and can be looked at as two different events. If they are right next to each other, chances are they're related to each other.

Determine the timing of an event or occurrence. To figure out the timing within a week, mentally divide the cards in half. That gives you a rough two weeks in each half. Then mentally divide the cards again, leaving four quarters, or four weeks. You may see a trip in the second week of the month. Not every week is going to have a big event in it, it's okay not to see something in every week —whatever comes up is what is supposed to come up.

Add the descriptions. The words directly on either side of the people or event most likely go with that person or event. Occasionally they may be mixed up and you'll have to move them around a bit. Once you see what you are working with, it may be obvious that the last card should be matched with the first card, and you can move it there.

Now read the upside-down cards. Before you begin speaking, make a note of the cards that are upside down and the ones that are right side up.

Cards that are facing the right direction are read the way they are written. Cards that are reversed are read several ways.

For a backward *word* card. You can either read it as the opposite of what is written, or you could say that there is an unseen problem blocking the word from being right side up. Let's say the word is "happy": You can either look at it as meaning sad and disappointed, or as meaning that your friend could be happy with this experience but there is something blocking her happiness. You may even be able to tell her what that something is by looking at the rest of the cards or using your psychic abilities.

If an *event* or a *person* is upside down: There can be a problem with the planning of it, it won't turn out the way they think it will, or the energy of the event is blocked. If the card is "romantic date," you can tell your friend, "There'll be problems getting it together; it won't be as romantic as you want it to be"; or, "You might have a problem making it as romantic as you envision, so make sure you think of everything." Use your intuition to pick which one works best in each case.

Don't get me wrong, if something is upside

down, it can still be great, but the way it stands at the time of the reading, some effort has to be put into it to change the outcome. Feel free to say just these things in your reading—it'll give your friend something to think about.

Look for any astrology signs to round out the reading. The astrology signs are read a few ways. First, they can describe a person's birthday or what the person is like, or the characteristics of an event in that month, depending upon what cards they fall next to. Let's say Aries falls next to "cute guy": You can either say he is born in April, or that he is energetic and independent. If you need help figuring out the meanings of the different signs, look up *Astrology* in the Dictionary of Psychic Signs and Symbols at the back of the book.

Read the cards like you would read a story and add your intuition. Everything will fall into place when you connect the words and images into one story line. Depending upon how your psychic abilities work, you may want to study the cards or close your eyes and pick up information using your inner senses before you begin to speak. Take your time and figure out how you work best when reading this way for others.

When you are finished, move on to the next month!

Confused? Here's an example of a birthday reading. I've given many to friends; the only difference is that I use tarot cards, but they have very similar meanings to the ones you've just written. In one month, the six cards were: an invitation, a young man who was a Leo (upside down), delays, success (upside down), money, party.

This is how I read them: "The first week, your ex-boyfriend [my interpretation of the upside-down Leo] is going to call you and ask you to do something, but I don't think you're going to do it. Not much is going on in the middle of the month, it looks a little boring, but by the end of the month you have some big career project with money and you'll be celebrating big-time. It feels like something you've been trying for, that you can't get going, then toward the end of the month—boom! it just happens."

Your Scorecard

EVEN though you are giving the reading, this game is only half about your accuracy. How you present yourself, as the reader, is part of your score on this one.

Yes, you want to be correct, truthful, and inspiring, but since this is your friend's birthday present, you want to make sure she understands you and has a good time, too.

Don't worry so much about being right as about making your predictions in complete sentences. Even though you are not making up the information that's coming through, how you get that stuff across is up to you.

People love hearing about themselves, whether you end up being right or not. It's a big responsibility to read for someone, and as long as you keep this in mind, nothing else really matters. This reading is almost foolproof. Somehow the cards end up in the order that they are supposed to — it really works!

At the end of a few months, you can check back with your friend and see how much of what you said came true, and if the events you described happened in the right months.

I remember when I first started reading, my friends would always come up to me and say, "You know, everything you told me came true!" At first I didn't believe them, but now I do!

Psy-Tips

NOW that you are finished, you may have some questions about this that you didn't know you had before you began. Here are the biggies that everyone wants to know when they do their first birthday reading.

★ *How do I know that I am getting psychic information when I look at the cards?* The cards are just a tool, a magnifying glass for your abilities. They help you focus your energies in the right direction. The words and images on the cards mean nothing without your ability to read them. It's so obvious that you may not realize this, but it's true. The more you do it, the more you'll be able to infuse the reading with your intuition.

★ *What happens if I don't understand how some of them fit together?* Just say what you know and leave the rest for your friend to experience when she gets there. It's okay to admit that you don't really understand the whole picture. When I do a reading, if I see a bunch of random facts, I try my best to make sense out of them, but if I can't, I'll tell someone, "This doesn't make sense to me, but I'll just say it anyway."

Don't try and fudge your way through it just because I say so. No matter what aspect of the reading you are confused about, the truth is always the way to go.

★ *What do I do if I think something bad is going to hap-*

pen? Most likely you are not going to run into this problem. If you look at your life and the lives of people around you, for the most part they're content with what is going on with them. How often do people you know have bad things happen to them? Not very often. This same thing applies to your reading with your friend.

On the other hand, if you do feel that something bad is coming, you don't have to say everything. You know your friend and what they can handle. Sometimes it's better to keep things to yourself. Besides, you may be wrong, and why worry them unnecessarily?

★ *What if I didn't do a good job with the reading?* First of all, your friend probably loved it anyway, but if you didn't quite understand everything the first time around, you can always do it again. This is a new skill, and like everything else, it may take some practice. Don't think that if you didn't understand it all in a snap there is something wrong.

When I first started, sometimes I'd be stretched to the limit trying to find a way to say something that would make sense; trying to find something intuitive to say about a card that said "travel." Where? With whom? After a while I was able to supply these details. The more you do it, the better you'll become.

[RING RING]
IT'S YOUR INTUITION CALLING!

EVERYONE'S seen ads for the psychic hotlines — you may have even tried one of them. Whether you've called one or not, I bet you didn't know how easy it is to use your psychic abilities over the phone. You see, your psychic ability instantly connects you to something beyond the physical world, so your intuition isn't limited to the immediate environment like your other five senses are. That means you can do it under any circumstance — including long distances. In other words, you're already a phone psychic — you just don't know it.

Rules of the Game

THIS game challenges one of the biggest misconceptions about psychic abilities, that you have to be in the same room as the person you are reading for your intuition to work. This may be hard to understand until you try it for yourself, but after you have developed your sixth sense, you'll be able to do it almost anywhere.

This opens up a whole new world to you. Now instead of just practicing your intuition with your friends who live close by, you can do it with people who live on the other side of the country. If you spend a lot of time on the phone anyway, then this should come naturally to you.

There are several ways to use your abilities over the phone. You can play one of the games you've already played, like the Sending and Receiving telepathy game from earlier in the chapter, except instead of beaming the images across the table, you're beaming them across greater distances. You didn't have to touch each other to receive the message that time, and you don't for this, either.

Another way you can use your intuition over the phone is to talk to your friend's angels like you did for yourself in Angelic Inspirations in chapter 2. You pose a question for her, and simply feel the angels' answers streaming through the phone and write them down as she waits on the other end. When you are finished, read her the message—I'm sure she'll be impressed.

The third way you can read over long distances is with your own set of guidance cards. Make your own guidance cards, the same ones you made for your friend in the birthday reading. When you are on the phone, take a moment to turn on your psychic abilities and ask your friend what she wants to know. Throw down five or six to answer the question and read them the same way you read a month in a birthday reading.

Those ways are all fun, but we're going to concentrate on another technique for this game. We're going to do what I call *symbol readings*. That's when you concentrate on the person you are reading and wait for an image or symbol to appear in your mind's eye and then use it to guide your reading. It's like a psychic inkblot test, like how your mind sees pictures in those big splotches of black ink.

Close your eyes, breathe deeply, and bring your awareness to your connection to your friend. Feel her close to you just as easily as you can hear her in your ear. When you feel that your connection is set, concentrate on your third eye area, or your mind's eye, the place where you see psychic impressions. Focus actively and wait for a symbol or an image to form there.

When you first play this game, you need to work out the meanings of each image as it comes up. After you've done it a few times, you start understanding how your intuition works with symbols and it won't be a challenge to figure things out. Also, the more you do it, the more you'll find instant information coming along with the picture to tell you what it is and what it's all about.

Try this over the Internet to take your instant messages to a whole new level. It's not much different from the phone, only when you are describing the symbols, you just have to type as fast as you think or you might lose your train of thought.

PLAY THE GAME:
BE A PHONE PSYCHIC

Pick a friend to call. Make it someone who would be excited about having a reading, who is also sympathetic to your psychic experimenting. It should be a friend who you are comfortable with but not someone you know inside and out. With people you know *really* well, sometimes it can be hard to tell the difference between what you know and what you psychically see. Schedule a specific time to do your psychic phone reading, and block off 15–20 minutes. Tell your friend to write out a couple of questions they want to look into.

Start 15–20 minutes before the reading. Relax, light some candles, burn some sage. Close your eyes, breathe deeply, and activate your inner senses. Keep your notebook around, just in case you want to draw or write something while you are in session. You can keep your candles burning during the reading if you like. When you are ready, call your friend from a quiet room.

Don't talk too much before you start. Tell them what you are going to do and ask them if they are ready. Tell them to please be quiet while you are concentrating and to be patient because it may take a few minutes to get going.

Open to your psychic flow. Close your eyes, breathe deeply, and bring your awareness to your connection to your friend. Feel her close to you just as you can hear her in your ear. When you feel like your connection is set, concentrate on your third eye area, or your mind's eye, the place where you see psychic impressions.

Experience being psychic. Focus actively and wait for a symbol or an image to form there. If you are clairaudient, you can concentrate on your mind's eye or your inner ear to hear a word that identifies a symbol, or if you are a feeling person, concentrate on your mind's eye and feel what is there as if you are looking at an image behind a black curtain.

Begin by describing what you hear, say, and feel. As you start talking about it, the image will become clearer. This image is either something that is in her life right now or is a symbol for something going on in her life right now. When you've gotten a rough image, ask your friend if it makes sense to her. She will either say yes or no.

If she answers yes. If she says yes, you can find out why by concentrating on that image and asking yourself, "How is it directly related to her life?" Another image will pop up. Keep describing what you see and feel until you have a clear image. Based on the things you've just said, guess why you think that image is relevant to her life. Ask her for feedback.

If she answers no. If she says no, then that means the image you see has a symbolic meaning instead of a literal one. Here's what you do: Concentrate on that image and ask yourself, "How does this symbol translate into her real life?" Yet again, another image will pop up. Describe what you see and feel until you have a better understanding of how that symbol relates to her life, then guess based on what you feel.

Do the same thing with one of the questions on her list. Just concentrate on her question, watch for an image or a feeling to pop up, and take it from there.

End the session. Stop when you feel tired or begin to disconnect. Talk about the reading with your friend, and write about it in your notebook.

Your Scorecard

JUST talking to your friend will give you a good idea of how many things you said that really struck home. Even if you only nailed a few the first time around, that should be enough to excite you and get you to try again. Since your intuition has a symbol dictionary all its own, the more you do it, the easier it becomes.

If you want a more specific accuracy rate, you can have your friend write down or tape-record every prediction. Give yourself two points for every bull's-eye statement, one point for every prediction that's in the ballpark, and zippo for the incorrect ones.

Since the rules of this game encourage you to talk it through, don't add to the official number any statements you make while you are rummaging through your psychic brain. When you first receive a symbol, you have to think about it to develop your impressions; you may say conflicting things while you do this. Don't use those musings to get an accuracy rate. When you are ready, and everything makes sense, you can then restate, for the record, any information you received during that time. Any questions you ask your friend for feedback during the process are fair game.

★ ★ ★

Here's how to get your accuracy rate:

> Double the number of total predictions you made
> to get the perfect score.
> Add up all of your bull's-eye and in-the-ballpark
> points to get your score.
> Divide the perfect score by your score.
> Multipy that number by 100.

Don't search for an accuracy rate until after you've done this a bunch of times—even then, you should do this a few times and average out your score for the most accurate of accuracy rates.

Psy-Tips

PLAYING this game is like walking a tightrope without a net. It can be quite scary to search for images and try to apply meanings to them right in front of a friend. If you aren't seeing and feeling stuff right away, it's not because you can't do a symbol reading for a friend over the phone, it's that there's something blocking your access.

Maybe you became self-conscious or were afraid to say something wrong and then panicked and intuitively shut down. Maybe there were so many things flying though your brain that you couldn't concentrate. The only thing that is going to help is to relax. Relax, tune out your friend, tune out the buzz, and just make it about you and the symbol.

The first few times you do this, the number one thing you are trying to figure out is how to access accurate psychic information and get to know what that feels like. Try using each of your abilities and really give each one time to work. You can even ask your angels to guide you through the reading.

You are not here to impress your friend, just to develop and use your natural sixth sense. If you received two symbols at first, or two conflicting reasons for a symbol, explore it with your friend, ask her about them. Maybe one is her past and one is her present. Maybe one is a book she is currently reading, or maybe it's just plain wrong. Exploring things with her will give you a better idea of how you work and how you are most accurate.

PSYCHIC TOOLS YOU HAVE LYING AROUND YOUR HOUSE

You've heard of tarot cards and crystal balls, but you probably didn't know that things you have in your house are instruments for your psychic development.

★ **Bowl of water.** Soft-focus staring into a glass or bowl of water is called scrying. Get into a psychic state, then stare into the center of the water for as long as you can. If you are good at this, you'll see images in the water or in your quiet mind.

★ **Candles.** Make a psychic game out of lighting tapered candles and see what happens. The flames will reflect your psychic state. They'll become really tall and thin or really thick and flat. They'll flicker up and down and become surrounded by a three-inch sparkly vapor. You may see angels in the flames or in the smoke the candles let off.

★ **Necklace.** You can take any pendant and make it into a pendulum. We did this with The Love Psychic game in chapter 2. Hold it still between your thumb and forefinger and ask a yes or no question. It will slowly start to move. Clockwise means yes, counterclockwise means no.

★ **Tea bag.** Cut the tea bag and pour the tea leaves into about a half an inch of hot water and mix it well. Think about what you want to know and take a sip for good luck. Dump the water out into a saucer and study the granules you have left in the cup. Begin reading at the top and continue around clockwise. Focus on the images you see on the inside of the cup. Do you see bumps or smooth lines? Odd recognizable shapes? What pops into your mind as you see them? Use your intuition to read the signs.

★ **Mirror.** Some people find that they can easily see their angel and spirit guide over their left and right shoulder by staring into a mirror. Get into a psychic state. As you breathe deeply, focus on your eyes in the mirror and stare as long as you can. It is easier to see the outline of your guides and angels by not staring at them directly. From the corners of your eyes, what do you see?

A PICTURE SAYS A THOUSAND WORDS

IN psychic terms, this expression really is true. There is a way to look into someone's eyes in a picture and know what that person is like inside. It doesn't matter whether the photo is a good one or bad, the person is smiling or frowning—a picture captures their essence. Pick a friend, play this game, and you'll find out exactly how much you can see in a snapshot.

Game Pieces

BEFORE you and your friend begin, you need to gather some things:

Five or six manila envelopes
Blank and lined paper, separate from your note-
    book
Pens

Ask a third person for some photographs of people neither one of you know. Tell them to pick about five people that they know well. The people don't have to be alone in a photo—they can be taken at a family party or a special event, just make sure that the person's face is clear and they aren't wearing sunglasses.

Tell them to make sure they don't give you images of people who would absolutely be offended by this game. You could even have your friend call them and get their okay first. You don't want to be practicing on someone who would be uncomfortable.

PLAY THE GAME: PICTURE READINGS

Grab a friend and some photos of people you don't know. Sit on the same side of a table or side by side on the floor.

Quiet your mind. Close your eyes, take a few deep breaths, and awaken your inner senses.

Take out one of the photos and place it between you. Take one of the blank papers and cover the person's nose and mouth so you are just concentrating on the eyes. Both of you can take turns studying the image. After a few minutes a personality will start to form from within the eyes of the person.

Begin your picture reading. Look at the left eye, the pupil, the lid. What feeling does it evoke in you? It may seem sad, deep, emotional, closed-minded, bright—you may feel just about anything. The psychic ability at work here is your clairsentience, your *feeling* and *knowing* senses. Most likely, psychic information isn't going to hit you in the head; you are not going to close your eyes and see images or hear a stream of words in your head. Instead, you are going to have to rely on your first *feeling* and trust as your feelings take you through the different personality traits.

Discuss your intuitive impressions with each other. Most likely, you'll agree on what you see and feel, but there is always a chance that you'll have a difference of opinion. That's okay. Simply describe what you see and write it down on the paper.

Focus on to the right eye and do the same thing. Then take a look at what you've written already. These are the different characteristics of this person.

Discover the overall personality and how he or she operates in the world. Do this by focusing on both eyes or the entire face and ask yourselves the following questions:

How does this person feel about their friends, parents, siblings?

What is this person like as a friend, student, co-worker?

How do they interact with others?

What is their general outlook on life?

What is this person's hobbies and interests?

Discuss the answers with your friend and write them down. When you are finished, put the picture and the pages of information in an envelope and move on to the next photo.

Do this with pictures of a couple. Look at their eyes in a photo and concentrate on the following questions:

What is the dynamic at work here?

How do they interact together?

How does he feel about her?

How does she feel about him?

Stop when you get tired or bored. When you are finished, go find your friend and score the game.

Your Scorecard

GIVE the person who gave you the pictures a red pen. Sit down with them and go over your notes. Let them go through and circle the things you got right and put question marks by the things that they are unsure of. Have them cross off the predictions that are wrong. Make sure that only the predictions that are absolutely wrong are crossed off or tell your friend just to put a question mark next to them. Sometimes people don't know everything about the people in their lives. You could be right as easily as you could be wrong and your friend may just not know it.

Look at the overall marks on the page. If less than a third of them are crossed off and more than a third are circled, you played this game well. Don't be surprised if you read one image better than another—you'll get better in time.

Psy-Tips

WITH this kind of game it can be hard to get started, but it gets much easier once you find your flow. It may help if you construct a sentence and answer as best you can, something like, "I feel this person is_____," or, "Emotionally, this person is____."

If that doesn't help right away, don't panic. It may take you a few tries before you have that inner-eye-opening *ah-ha* experience. If you're not sure of yourself—and that is common for a first-timer—then force yourself to say something, anything. You may not be comfortable, but hey, it's a start!

Also, remember that just because you're not feeling anything doesn't mean you're automatically getting wrong information. And really, you don't know what it feels like—so don't automatically think you're not feeling anything! You truly don't know if you are right or wrong until you come face-to-face with someone who knows that person in the picture.

People are either good at this game or not. Your friend might have gotten it right away, while you may have to work at it a bit. Understanding that *feeling* is a very subtle thing, it becomes a lot easier with practice.

HOW DO A COUPLE OF PSYCHICS GET READY FOR A PARTY?

The answer? By taking this psychic party test, of course! All you need is a friend, a notebook, and a big night out.

The day of your next party, you and a friend grab your notebooks and sit quietly for about ten minutes. Your goal? To write down everything that is going to happen during the party before it occurs.

You can do this together or separately, whichever works better for you. Close your eyes, take a few deep breaths, and activate your psychic abilities. First use your inner sight, your clairvoyance. Concentrate on the area of your forehead above your eyes and bring yourself to your party. What will happen? See everything: What is the host wearing? Who is going to show up late? Who is flirting with who? Write it all down.

After the images have all played out, use your clairsentience. Concentrate on your feeling and knowing senses. Feel your whole body at the party and sense what is going to happen. Ask yourself questions like: Who will be there? Who is talking to who? What are they talking about? Are there any surprises throughout the night? As the answers hit you, jot them down.

Now it's time to move on to your clairaudient hearing senses. Focus on your inner ears and ask your angels, spirit guides, or your psychic self a question in your mind and find out what is going to happen that way. *Who am I going to be chatting with? What will we be chatting about? What will happen between me and my sweetie? How can I get him alone tonight?* Write down the stream of words that you hear and feel.

Put all of your notes in an envelope. When you get to the party, swap envelopes with your psychic partner in crime and enjoy yourselves. At the end of the night, open the envelopes and see how much you knew in advance. Who had more correct predictions? You get the gold star!

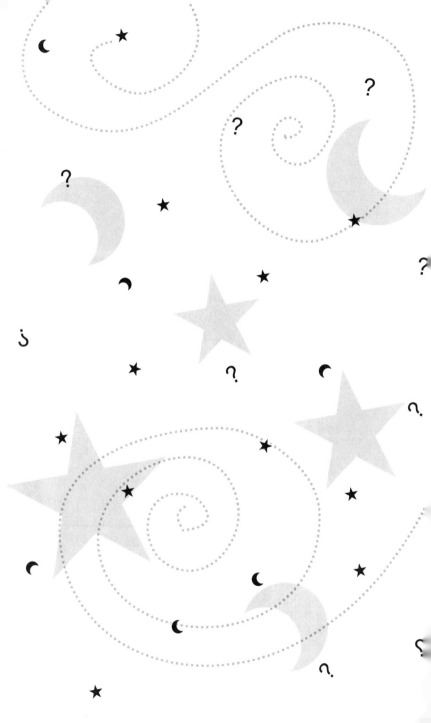

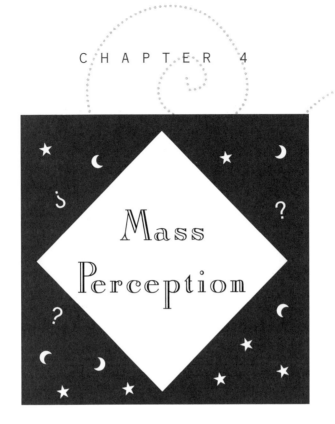

CHAPTER 4

Mass Perception

Psychic Party Games!

THE next time you're getting together with friends, don't watch a movie or hang around the mall—play psychic games! There is a ton of psychic power in groups. It's true, wild and bizarre things happen when people get together to focus on their inner senses, and that is definitely more interesting than haunting the park after dark.

The games in this chapter cover a whole load of cool things. There's *Tag Team Telepathy*, in which you split off into teams, go to different locations, and see through each other's eyes. And the *Psychic Circle*, where you get together with friends and focus on mysterious items in an envelope. You can have an *Angel Séance* to call on your otherworldly assistants, and tap into the power of the moon with the *Full Moon Psychic Ceremony*. There's even an ESP quiz, as well as some fun guessing games (hint: one includes chocolate, the other, presents!).

Even though the games in this chapter work with the same abilities the other chapters do, the fact that you're doing them in groups of three or more will have quite an impact on the effectiveness of your skills. This is because when a group of people get psychic together, no matter how big or small the group, it brings out the unconscious psychic abilities of all the people involved. You are able to do things you just can't do alone. So if you struggled to receive information when you were watching Intuition Television alone, or couldn't quite make out the details when you played the telepathy games with a friend, you'll have a much different experience with these games.

Somehow everyone's skills are magnified when they focus on the same thing at the same time. You don't have to be using the same psychic ability or sending and receiving the same thought—just that you are doing the stuff together, that's the magic key. So as you go through the games in this chapter, don't be surprised if your accuracy rate jumps up a few notches.

The other good thing about doing psychic games in groups is that you have plenty of people to talk to after you're finished. When you were alone and something really cool happened, you might not have had anyone to tell. With these games, you'll always have people that will be seeing, hearing, and feeling the same out-of-this-world stuff that you do, and nobody will think you're crazy, either.

Now that you're prepared to open new psychic doorways, pick one of these games, invite some good friends, and have a psychic sleepover party.

TAG TEAM TELEPATHY: A REMOTE VIEWING GAME

THIS is a great game to develop your sixth sense and test your telepathy. In a nutshell, here's how it works: One team of friends is out, *sending* around town; the other team is receiving at home, looking through their eyes and seeing what they see. It's an amazingly accurate game. By the time the sending team comes home, the receivers have detailed descriptions and drawings of where they have been. Bet you didn't know you could be in the park without ever leaving your house!

Rules of the Game

ONCE you decide to play this game and separate into teams, everything's got to be a secret. The sending team cannot hint to the receiving team where they are going. You don't even want any observers to know. That way, you'll know that no one can help the receiving team with a glance in a certain direction, by pointing a finger, or by telepathically giving them information that should only come from the sending team.

It is best to play this game during the day or even at dusk—not after the sun has gone down, or you won't be able to see anything. The only tools you'll need are a sketch pad or a notebook, and some pencils and pens. You can have a tape recorder around to record every prediction on tape, but that's up to you.

The game works best with four people, but can be done with more. If you have six people you can have one sending team and two receiving teams—just put the two receiving teams in different rooms or locations. If you have an odd number of people, you can have two controlled observers on each team.

PLAY THE GAME:
TAG TEAM TELEPATHY

Divide up four people into teams of two. One is the sending team and one the receiving team. One member of the sending team is going to be the controlled observer and one is going to be the sender. One member of the receiving team is going to be the controlled observer and the other the psychic receiver. Don't tell the other team which one of you is the control and which one is the sender or receiver.

Set a time to begin the game, and separate. The start time should be at least an hour from the current time. Before start time, the receiving team goes to a quiet place where they can be alone.

The sending team's control leads the sender around town. It doesn't matter whether you are driving, walking, biking, or blading. What's important is that the sender does not know where you are going and how you're going to get there—they are just along for the ride.

The sending team should be at their location by the appointed time. The sender's control then chooses what direction the sender will look in. You could decide together, but it should be one general direction. You don't want the sender to send so much conflicting information that it confuses the receiver.

Here's an example, just so it's crystal clear. Let's say you end up in a fast-food restaurant. If you walk around the whole place soaking up everything, the receiver will see cars, a parking lot, tables, cash registers, mops, uniforms—it's just too much. To avoid this, stop in one location and look in one general direction, like in the parking lot facing the restaurant, or sitting at a table viewing the front door.

The controls for both sides tell the sender and receiver when to begin. The sender looks around, slowly studying the area in great detail.

At the same time, the receiver gets into a psychic state and describes the area to the control. Use the notebooks to write and to draw maps and pictures of what you see, hear, or feel. Do this for 15–20 minutes.

Both teams meet up to discuss what happened. After you've talked about it, bring the psychic receiver to the location to see what it looks like and compare it with the information that was received.

Your Scorecard

WHEN you meet up afterward, the receiving team begins by describing the impressions they received and, based on that information, guessing where they were. After the receiving team has had their shot, the sending team clarifies the details.

When it is all over, go back to the location to clear up any mysteries. The receiver can easily pick up information the sender isn't aware of. If the receiver had the impression the sender was standing near a tire mark, but the sending team doesn't remember that detail, you may all think the receiver was wrong—unless both teams go back and check it out.

Psy-Tips

THERE can be a lot of pressure on the psychic receiver in this game. Instead of stressing, make sure you've practiced Your First Psychic Adventure in chapter 1, maybe even some of the games in chapter 2, so that you're comfortable getting into receiving mode. Basically your goal is to get into your friend's mind and see through her eyes. To do this, you visualize your friend standing at the location: What are you looking at? You can put yourself into your friend's body and *feel* the surroundings.

Every psychic has their own method of getting information, and it may take you a bit of time to figure out yours. Some people find that it is easier to describe what they see out loud; that's where the control and a tape recorder come in handy. Other people let the images stream from their psychic senses right into drawings and written words. If you do it this way, make sure you describe the details of the images to the control when you are finished or write notes around your pictures before the senders come home.

You can also try asking yourself or your angels some questions: *If I was there, what would I see? Where is my friend and what is she looking at? Is it cold? Is it sunny? Is it green, blue? Is there tons of concrete or glass around?* Your controlled observer can ask you some of the above questions as well.

If you are having problems getting started, force yourself to blurt out anything. Sometimes psychic impressions are like a train: One car follows another, one image follows another. Once you get the flow moving, it'll be easier to get more impressions—the first one is always the most difficult.

If you are seeing two conflicting pictures, and you don't know which one to choose, describe them both. There are many reasons why you can see a few things. Your unconscious could be exerting itself some way, you could be wrongly associating one place with the other, or you could just be wrong. On the other hand, you may be seeing the current location and the area the sending team was an hour before this, which is actually really accurate. The bottom line here: Don't stress yourself out over choosing one or the other, because there is plenty of time to describe both.

If you've tried all these tips and you're still not comfortable, there is one more thing you can try. It's softening the rules a bit, but not breaking them. If the sender and receiver have a hard time connecting, you can take some of the secrecy out of the game by letting the group know who the sender is. That gives the receiver a chance to telepathically connect before the two teams separate and begin the game.

CHOCOLATE PARTY GAMES

Did you know that M&M's are great testers of psychic ability? Get the mini bags, the ones that have about 10 candies individually wrapped, and give them out at your party. Have your friends carefully open the packages without being able to see what's inside. Tell them to close their eyes and guess what color M&M they are about to pick out. They can have their fingers on one candy, but they must blurt out a color before they pull it out.

This also works with chocolate that has a message in the wrapper, such as Dove chocolates. Inside the red-and-blue-wrapped chocolates is a fortune or word of wisdom; before you open it, hold the candy in your hand and guess what the fortune is about.

You can also take five to ten different types of candy bars and put them all in a big paper bag (make sure they're each prewrapped, or this could be gross). Reach inside and take hold of one of the chocolates. Ask your friends to guess which candy you have in your hands. If they are right, they get to eat it; if not, they don't get one! That'll give them some incentive to keep up the psychic work.

CREATING A PSYCHIC CIRCLE: ANOTHER REMOTE VIEWING GAME

REMOTE viewing is the psychic spy stuff the CIA used to get information on top-secret bombs and see inside buildings. Since they weren't doing this just for fun, they followed very specific protocols. Those scientific standards made them absolutely sure that the info they were getting was only from their psychic ability—not from telepathy, not from their unconscious, not from their memory. These steps are easy to follow; it's not as technical as it sounds. Play this game and you'll end up with great results.

Game Pieces

TO play this game you need:

> Manila envelopes for each person in the group (6-by-9 or larger)
> Larger manila envelopes to put the first ones into (9-by-12 or larger)
> A parent, sibling, or friend not in the group to help you prepare for the game
> A notebook and pen
> An alarm clock or timer

Give each person in the group the same smaller-size envelope, the kind you absolutely cannot see through. Each person should have a parent or sibling put some interrelated information in it, such as a picture and a birth certificate of your grandmother; a few articles and photos of a famous person; a menu and a receipt from a restaurant; a map from a park. Whatever it is, it all has to relate to the same subject.

Make sure they know the envelope must stay pretty flat. Three or four documents is fine. You also don't want something really large in there that doesn't fit right, or it might be a giveaway. In other words, an old key chain is out of the question. Also, tell them not to put anything private in the envelope; before the party is over, everyone's going to know what's in there.

The biggest rule: No one may know what that family member has put in the envelope — so don't even ask them!

After the envelopes are made, each member of the group should keep theirs in a safe place so that it gets no identifying dirt or creases on it. Everyone needs to bring their envelope, notebook, and pen with them when they come to the party.

Rules of the Game

GET a group of people together and give them each a smaller-size envelope. Go over the rules with them and make sure they understand how their parent or friend is supposed to prepare the envelope. Set a time and date for your party a bit in advance so that you give everyone a chance to have their envelopes filled with some good stuff, not just whatever is easiest to find.

PLAY THE GAME: PSYCHIC CIRCLE

Tell people to prepare their envelopes in advance. As people enter the party, put their envelopes into the bigger manila envelopes. This should guarantee that no matter what is in one envelope, it cannot be distinguished from another. Keep all the envelopes in a pile. As envelopes get added to the pile, mix them up so that there is no chance anyone would know which one is theirs.

Sit in a circle with the envelopes in the center and quiet your minds. Close your eyes, take a few deep breaths, and quiet your mind. Choose

154

one of the envelopes. Leave it in the center and put the other ones aside. Set a timer for 15 minutes.

Get into a psychic state. As a group, focus on your breathing or listen to meditation music for a few minutes. Focus your concentration on the envelope and get as much information as you can about the subject. Don't worry if you are right or wrong or how the things are connected, just write down everything you see, hear, and feel.

If you've done this before, you know which of the senses you like best. Clairvoyants can focus on your mind's eye and see inner images of what is in the envelope or pictures relating to the information. Write or draw what you see. If you are clairsentient, feel yourself connecting to the envelope—even feel yourself inside the envelope— and write down everything that pops into your mind. Clairaudients can ask their angels or psychic selves to describe what is inside the envelope and describe any other information they need to make sense of it.

End your game. When the timer goes off, finish writing, share your notes, open the envelope, and see who won.

Your Scorecard

WHEN the time is up and everyone is done, share your notes. See if you can make sense of what is in the envelope as a group before you open it. Once you know what is inside, see who was right. You can even find a winner by counting up how many right and wrong things were said.

Don't worry if you don't get it right away. With this exercise you can really nail it or completely bungle it. If two or three out of the group get it, you're doing all right. Even the CIA guys had it wrong sometimes.

Psy-Tips

THE point of this game is that you're not supposed to have the slightest clue as to what is in the envelope, and that can be kind of scary. If you don't get brilliant flashes of insight right away, don't bug out, take a guess. Playing psychic games is just like guessing — except that you're right a lot. Writing down one thing makes it easier to write another, and another — that's the way you get a flow going. This may take a few tries to understand, so if you get it wrong the first time, try again.

If you got conflicting pieces of information, write

down everything and don't try to make sense out of it. You might be getting two scenarios, and you automatically think one of them is wrong. Since you can't figure out which one is right, you don't write down either of them. Stop judging the information that comes through; they could actually be connected somehow and you just don't know it. Think about this when writing down everything you see, hear, and feel. You might get something wrong, but you'll most definitely get something right, too.

Here are some tips that will help you get to the juicy psychic stuff more easily. See yourself opening the envelope and write down what you feel is inside. Or concentrate on the envelope in your mind's eye, bringing your awareness into the envelope and looking around—what's inside? You can even ask yourself and your angels some choice questions: *Is this about a person, place, or thing? What can you tell me about the stuff in the envelope? Is it living or dead? Old or young? Near or far?*

PSYCHIC TREASURE HUNT

DID you ever go to a party, look around and see who is the best dressed, who is the cutest, and who is the funniest? Now you can also find out who at the party is the most psychic. The next time you have a party, give everyone this psychic pop quiz — see who gets the most answers right.

Game Pieces

HERE are the things you are going to need to create the ESP quiz:

    10 business envelopes
    20 sheets of blank paper
    A pen
    One larger envelope in which the smaller ones easily fit into
    Notebooks or separate sheets of paper to keep track of the answers and scores
    An inexpensive but very cool prize for the winner!

Someone at the party is going to be giving the test. This person needs to ask one of their parents or friends to help create it. Make sure the person you ask doesn't know anyone at the party, and don't tell anyone who created the test until after you're finished. It's important not to create the test yourself, or you could unconsciously be thinking the answers out loud to anyone who can hear with their inner ear!

Give the following instructions to the test maker.

Making the Test

THE writer of the test is in charge of coming up with the answers that the test takers are going to psychically search for. Write down the following nine items on nine different sheets of paper. You can write the first thing that comes to your mind, or you can think about it for a while. Since question #10 doesn't require an answer in advance, you don't have to worry about that one.

Write each answer on its own sheet of paper and fold it into a second sheet. Put each of the answers in a different business-size envelope. Label the envelopes on the outside with the number and the description in the order below. Put the nine smaller envelopes inside the bigger one. This makes it very easy for the person giving the test to take each envelope, hold it in front of the group, and ask them what is written inside.

Make the tie-breaker envelope the same way you do the rest.

#1 Write down a color of the rainbow
#2 A letter of the alphabet
#3 Draw a simple everyday image (house, shoe, car, etc.)
#4 Write a number from 0 to 9

#5 A zoo animal (gorilla, snake, tiger — not something rare like a lemur, okay?)

#6 A current television show

#7 One of the 50 states

#8 A denomination of money (penny, dime, quarter, dollar, five-dollar bill, etc.)

#9 A popular song

#10 Name the person at this party who is going to win this test!

Tie-breaker: Draw a simple pattern containing two geometric shapes.

Make sure you don't share your answers with anyone, whether they are taking the test or not. You don't want to psychically influence the test.

Rules of the Game

THE way this test is set up now, it's testing pure psychic abilities: feeling, hearing, and seeing. You can easily make it a telepathy test by opening up the envelopes, one at a time, and actively sending the answer to everyone around you.

THE TEST:
PSYCHIC PARTY POP QUIZ

Make the test envelopes. Look at them before the test to make sure they are made correctly.

Gather the partygoers together and quiet your minds. Turn off the music, and give them each a piece of paper and a pen. Tell them to close their eyes, take a few deep breaths, and quiet their minds. This is serious business—you can't get psychic information with a mind full of buzz-buzz, so no joking, giggling, peeking, whispering, or tickling (save that stuff for afterward!).

Give everyone instructions. Tell them to focus on their mind's eye for a few moments and give a good psychic guess. Encourage the testers to write down any information that comes through describing the answer. They may not be able to get an exact name, but if they write down a few sentences that identify the answer perfectly, they can still score some points.

Hold up the first envelope. Read the question written on the side of the envelope. Give them a moment of silence and tell them to write down the first thing that comes into their mind. Go through each of the nine envelopes:

- #1 Write down a color of the rainbow
- #2 Draw a geometric shape
- #3 Draw a simple everyday image (house, shoe, car, etc.)
- #4 Write a number from 0 to 9
- #5 A zoo animal
- #6 A current television show
- #7 One of the 50 states
- #8 A denomination of money (coin or bill)
- #9 A popular song

Ask the tenth question:
#10 Name the person at this party who is going to win this test!

Depending upon everyone's different abilities, they can either visualize an image, hear a name or an initial, or feel what part of the room this person is sitting in.

Gather up the test papers. Make sure everyone has their name written on their test and gather them up. Score them and see who wins.

Give out the prize!

Your Scorecard

NOT every answer on the test is the same level of difficulty. Some of the questions are a lot easier to get right than others. Picking a color of the rainbow gives you a 12.5 percent chance of being correct, while you have only a 2 percent chance of naming the correct state.

The testers are not going for a high percentage of accuracy as much as they are trying to win, so it doesn't matter that some of these questions will be guessed wrong most of the time. If they want a pretty number, tell them to take one of the accuracy rate tests in chapter 2 or 3.

Here's how to score: Every spot-on correct answer gets two points. A near miss gets one point, and a wrong answer gets nothing—zippo. Right and wrong are easy to determine, so let's go over what makes a near miss.

Let's say the question is "Draw a simple everyday image," and the image in the envelope is a side view of a car with two wheels. If someone has a picture of two wheels except instead of a car, it's a wagon or a bicycle, then that's a near miss. And it's worth one point. Depending upon how closely their drawing resembles the image in the envelope, you may want to give it the full two points even if it's not 100 percent exact.

If a tester doesn't have the exact answer, but has three or four sentences that show you they got a handle on what it was, you can give them one or even two points, depending upon how accurate and specific the statements are.

If the question is "Write down a state in America," and the answer is Louisiana, and someone guessed the state wrong, but wrote, "Southern part of the country, near the Mississippi River," or drew a picture that looked almost exactly like Louisiana, then you can give them some credit for these correct statements. When you do this, make sure you are consistent — playing favorites is not allowed!

If there is a tie, go to the tie-breaker question. Draw a simple pattern with two geometric shapes. The one who draws the image the closest to correct wins. If both drawings are alike, the person with the most exact correct answers wins.

Psy-Tips

IT can be scary to have to make psychic predictions in front of other people. Anyone who has ever taken a test knows the added pressure, so the first thing is to relax. Don't let your focus be split by wondering how you are doing or whether the person next to you is more accurate than you are.

Those people who have been taking the tests all along are going to know the best way to receive their answers; they know whether they are naturally visual, hearing, or feeling people. Chances are that partygoers just along for the ride might be a little confused when it comes to picking information out of a hat. If you are unsure how to get psychically started, you may want to read the five basic steps described in chapter 1: Set your goals, quiet your mind, turn on your psychic faucet, experience being psychic, and end your session.

Even if you've never done so before, knowing where to concentrate your attention in your mind to use your inner seeing, hearing, and feeling senses will take the mystery out of the whole thing. You may get a bit confused the first time around, but at least you'll understand what you're doing.

ANGEL SÉANCE

EVERYONE has seen the movie version of an old-fashioned séance: a table with a crystal ball, a zany-looking woman with lots of makeup, long nails, and velvet wrapped around her head. That makes for good drama, but séances don't happen like this in the real world. You can get together with friends and do them the right way. Here's a simple and fun game where you contact each other's angels and get all sorts of enlightening messages—without the crystal ball, smoke, and mirrors.

Game Pieces

BEFORE you begin your séance, you need:

One candle for each person playing
A secure candleholder for each candle
One angel picture or statuette for each person
Incense or a sage smudge stick (optional)
Notebooks or pads and pens for each person to
  take angel notes

Rules of the Game

HERE'S an overview of what you'll be doing. You're going to sit in a circle with your candle and angel picture or statuette in front of you. The leader is going to say an angelic invocation and invite your angels to join you. You'll light your candles, hold hands, breathe deeply, and focus on the center of the circle. Then you go around the circle talking to angels and either repeating what you hear or writing down a message.

Before you start, let's talk about the difference between this séance and other ones. People use the power of groups in search of all sorts of out-of-this-world experiences. Whether you believe it or not, people try to talk to dead relatives and pets, spirit guides, aliens, dead celebrities, and—every year since his death—Houdini. (I don't think they've had any luck with him yet.)

When you go wandering around the ethers for those kind of spirits, you never know what you're getting into. The mysteries of the universe always fascinate people, but they can get them in trouble, too. That's why Ouija boards got such a bad rap. If you don't know how to use them correctly, you might not always have good experiences. You want to make sure you're playing with friends—even if you can't see them.

This séance is guaranteed to be entertaining and enlightening. Angels are all full of love and light; there is nothing bad about 'em. Talking to them is always uplifting. They love to play games, and whenever you connect to them you'll be sure to have a good time with lots of giggles.

You never know what's going to happen when you do an Angel Séance. You may feel angels packed in the circle, see colors or lights flying around the room, or just feel a sense of peace. You can get some fun messages, too. One time we got together I couldn't stop laughing. I kept thinking I was ruining everyone's concentration, I kept laughing and laughing, it was as if I were being tickled!

PLAY THE GAME: ANGEL SÉANCE

Gather a group of friends and pick a leader. Sit in a circle with your candle and angel picture or statue in front of you.

The leader lights the incense and recites the angelic invocation. Walk around the room and make sure the smoke fills the whole space while they speak these words:

Angelic Invocation

As we begin tonight, we take this moment to release any fears that may stop us from having a fun experience. Fill this room with only the purest sources of love and light. Let our angels from the highest realms be present as we play this game. Everything that happens during our Angel Séance is directly guided by these angels from heaven. With that said, we call on all the angels and the archangels that wish to hang out with us this evening to join us in our circle.

Light your candles and quiet your mind. Hold hands as you breathe deeply and focus on the center of the circle. You may feel a chill or see the candle flames flicker. That is when you know the angels are present with you. Once you know the angels are around, you can continue to hold hands or not—it's up to you.

One by one, each person gets an opportunity to listen for a message and repeat what they hear. You can either determine who will go first ahead of time, or you can go by who feels like going first once you get into it. If you do it that way, whoever feels the most comfortable with their clairaudient abilities should start.

The first receiver gets a message. The first person to be the receiver listens with their inner senses for a message and repeats what they hear. They can also write or draw it, whichever they are more comfortable with.

The message can be for the person talking, another person in the group, or something about life in general. Each receiver can go around the room and have the angel give each person in the group a little reading and just repeat what you hear. As this is going on, the rest of the group should focus on the angels in the center of the circle and the message being received.

Go around the circle as each person gets an opportunity to get a message. The rest of the group should focus on the angels in the center of the circle while the receiver concentrates. Listen as the message is being received.

End the séance. Thank the angels for playing with you and send them home. Spend the rest of the night talking about your experiences and the messages you picked up.

Your Scorecard

YOU can't often check the accuracy of the messages you get in a séance. If the angel happens to say something specific that you can verify, more power to you, but that's not likely to happen.

You'll know you spoke to angels by answering a few simple questions. When you received your messages, did you feel good about them? When you talk about them with each other, are they all positive? If you answered yes to these questions, you had a successful séance.

It's easier to tell when you *haven't* contacted angels.

We went over this when you talked to your angels in chapter 2. Angelic advice and wisdom will always be loving and empowering, no matter what they are talking about. When you discuss your messages with each other, if you find one that is fearful or tells you to do something negative, don't believe it. You can always do another séance and ask again, or get a friend who hears them more easily than you do to help you.

Psy-Tips

THIS whole thing may sound a little overwhelming, listening to angels in front of a group of friends. What if nothing happens? It's a lot easier to be psychic in groups, so I wouldn't worry about it. You have a better chance of talking to your angels together than you do alone; that is, as long as you can get past the self-conscious part of the game. Close your eyes and bring your concentration inward, take as long as you need and forget there is anyone else there. They'll do the same for you.

Getting started is always the most difficult part. Ask the most practiced psychic to start off the receiving and that should help. If most of you didn't hear or feel anything, you can try getting individual messages at the same time, which is a little easier and much less self-conscious. Get into a psychic state, call in the angels, and then concentrate, as a group, on receiving personal messages at the same time, focusing on your mind's eye and writing down the messages instead of speaking them out loud.

Very often first-time messages are short and sweet, and can even sound a bit hazy. If you are disappointed in the outcome, try another séance. The more you do it, the easier it'll become. You can also practice the angel games in chapter 2 between now and then. If you can do it alone, it can only get better when you do it with a group.

MOON POWER TO YOU!

BEWARE the full moon (hum *Twilight Zone* music here)—people everywhere become unstable and werewolves come out all over Europe. Okay, maybe not, but there is definitely unconscious, psychic power in the full moon—and we might as well take advantage of it, right? After all, this is a psychic book.

Here is a fun ceremony that you can do, not only at full moon but at the new moon, too, to tap into the underlying psychic powers of the universe and get them to work for you.

Game Pieces

A candle and secure candleholder

A twig or small branch (better to have some green leaves still on it)

A few flowers (separate the petals in a bowl)

A large bowl of water

Salt

Paper or plastic cups (one for each person at the party)

Sage, a smudge stick, or incense

A wish list

WHEN you work with natural forces like this, it's best to make sure each of the four elements are present — earth, air, water, and fire. The candle and the air in the room take care of the fire and air elements; the twig symbolizes the earth; the water is the water; salt is for absorbing negativity; and the flower petals, in all of their beauty, represent you.

You'll also need a well-thought-out wish list of things you want to change and get rid of for the full moon ceremony; or a wish list of things you want to get, acquire, or accomplish for the new moon. For more about that, keep reading.

Wish List Making

MAKING the exact right list of goals is just as important to this game as asking the right questions was in chapter 2. Finding the perfect way to state what you want is a skill, and just so we're absolutely sure you'll get it right the first time, here's a few words on the subject.

Whether you are making a list of things you wish to change and get rid of, or making a list of goals and things you want to get, make it as specific as possible. Say you want more money. You could ask for more money and leave it at that, but that's kind of hazy and it might not help your cause very much. In addition to asking the moon for more moolah, you could also do some good, hard thinking and list all the ways more money can come to you.

When I say *all*, I mean it. Don't limit yourself to what is practical. You can find money on the street or in an old wallet; you can also get offered a cool part-time job. By writing down all the ways money can come to you, you're giving moon power more room to work.

You also want to write positive statements instead of wishy-washy wishes. *Wanting* more money and *having* a greater flow of money in your life are two different things. So instead of writing, "I want more money," write, "Thanks for giving me more money." That is a much more effective way of getting it. Asking for something is the first step toward getting it, and feeling like you have it already will just get it to you faster.

Whether your list includes love, romance, school, friends, or anything else, you can benefit from stating what you want to get rid of as much as what you want to add to your life. When we don't like something in our lives, we have negative thoughts about it, and these thoughts can stop us from making our wishes come true.

Back to the money example. If you feel like you don't have enough, in addition to wishing for more money, you can ask to get rid of the obstacles that get in the way of having it. You can work on releasing any negative ideas you have as well. All this will help you develop a new way of thinking and assist the moon in working its magic.

One last thing. I know this doesn't have much to do with actual list making, but it's worth a few paragraphs. That old saying "Watch what you wish for" is really, really true. Think about what you are asking for. You may want to be the class president of your school, but if you got what you wished for, would you be able to handle the job and your studies, as well as keep up all your sports and hobbies? Would it be enjoyable for you? Maybe not. If that's so, then think about what you *really* want and work on getting that instead.

Often we want something so big that it may take some time to build up to it. If that's the case with you, it's better to ask for something that gets you closer to your goal, but is totally within your comfort zone. If you ask for something that it too big and unrealistic, you may not get it at all, and then you'll just think this whole moon ceremony thing was a big waste of time.

Here's a good example of this. If you want the lead in the school play, then maybe you should also ask for your acting, singing, and dancing to be the best it can be and practice your head off, instead of just wanting the lead. That way, when you get it, you'll know your moon ceremonies helped prepare and guide you, and you won't just feel like you won the leading-lady lottery and you're not able to handle it.

Writing the best list is only half of the game; the other half is what you *do* with the list. To play with your heart and soul, to really mean it and feel it as you concentrate on each wish, is what tapping into lunar energy is all about.

Rules of the Game

BEFORE you begin, decide whether you are doing this at the full moon to get rid of stuff, or the new moon to get things you want. The perfect thing is to do both. That will really get the out-with-the-old, in-with-the-new energy working overtime!

The full moon is when the moon is at its biggest, and the new moon is when it's at its smallest. Many calendars will tell you when there is a new and full moon, so just look it up and schedule your party for that day or evening. When planning, make sure the moon is totally full or new — it has to be after it begins to get the full effect. Have everyone make their list in advance.

PLAY THE GAME: FULL MOON PSYCHIC CEREMONY

Schedule your party. Decide to do this at the full moon to get rid of stuff, or the new moon to get things you want. Plan your party for that day or evening. Have everyone make their list in advance.

Place all the elements on a big table. Have everyone sit or stand around the table with some space in front of them. The leader lights the sage, smudge stick, or incense, and recites the Moon Ceremony Blessing as they wave it over all the elements on the table and fill the room with its scent.

Moon Ceremony Blessing

As we gather to perform our moon ceremony, we call to the light. We tap into the purest sources of energy to guide us and grant us our wishes.

Let the salt wash away any negativity.

Purify the water as it reflects the moon from the sky.

Bless the candle as it creates the warmth of fire for our ceremony.

Bless the branch and the earth as they bring our wishes to reality.

The petals we use to achieve our goals today remind us of all the beauty that is within us and our ability to make our dreams come true. Thank you.

Each person chooses their ceremonial items. A candle, a branch, some flower petals, and a cup. To prepare for the ceremony, touch the water and wipe it lightly over the candle, branch, and cup.

Set up your ceremonial space. Everyone puts a little salt in their cup, then a bit of water from the big bowl as they arrange their items in front of them however they want. Take out your lists, close your eyes, take a few deep breaths, and concentrate on the moon and its energy.

Bring your attention to the first thing on the list. Take a flower petal and hold it in your hands.

Repeat your request a few times as if you are telling it right to the moon. When you feel you have thought about it enough, put a drop of water on the petal and place it somewhere around your ceremonial space. Go down the items on your list and do the same thing until you are finished.

End the ceremony. Put your list under the candle or the cup of water and repeat the words "Thank you" several times as you again concentrate on the moon. Stretch and talk about your experience. Leave the candles burning after everyone is done and party for an hour or two, letting the ceremony continue as you hang out and have a good time.

When each person is ready to leave, put out your candle and take the ceremonial items home. Place them around your room to remind you of the things on your list. Keep your list in a safe place. In a few weeks or months you can look back at it and see how much your life has changed since you wrote it.

If you have a small party, here's another way you can do the ceremony. Make one ceremonial space using a bowl of water, and surround it with a few twigs and a few candles—as long as it's pretty, it doesn't matter how much of these items you use. Keep everything in the center of your circle or table. You and your friends can share the four elements as you perform the ceremony. If you do it this way, instead of having individual cups of water, you take a drop of water from the big bowl as you wish on each petal. It can be fun to do it all together.

Your Scorecard

YOU aren't working against anyone when you play this game, and you aren't trying to win. In fact, the reason why you do this with a group—besides having fun—is so that everyone's positive power rubs off on everyone else and makes the wishes come true better, faster, and more often. You don't all have to have the same goals for this to occur, you just have to do it together.

You can tell if you connected by how you felt during the game. Were you easily able to focus on your goals? Did you feel chills or a sense of peace when you were concentrating on the items on your list? Did you feel a bond with your friends as you worked together?

If you like concrete results, you'll have to wait at

least a few weeks to see how the things on your list come about, but if you answered yes to the questions above, then you are sure to see changes in your life, thanks to the moon.

Psy-Tips

DON'T judge your performance by the way other people did the moon ceremony. Some people feel things and others don't. Even if you didn't feel much different while you were performing the ceremony, that doesn't mean the things on your list won't come true.

Moon energy is subtle energy. You may not have developed enough psychic ability to feel it yet—but you don't have to feel it to make it work. To add oomph to the ceremony you just did, light your candle and focus on the items on your list every day for a week. You can even leave the candle lit while you do your homework or surf the Net—that way it'll keep working for you while you're doing something else.

After a few weeks, if you review your notes and not much came true, take another look at your goals. Are there things on the list that are too big to get in one shot? Do you have any fears or negative thoughts about any of the items on your list?

Rewrite your wish list and plan to do some more moon ceremonies—alone or with friends. This time, concentrate both on releasing any obstacles and achieving your goals. It just might take a few more sessions to get the energy working, but you'll soon see the results you are looking for.

GIFT GUESSING:
A PRIZEWINNING GAME!

HERE'S a gift game that blows Secret Santa out of the water. For this test, everyone invited needs to bring an inexpensive gift. Everyone at the party is going to use their intuition to guess what's in the box. The bottom line: The best psychics are going to take home the most gifts.

Game Pieces

TELL all the partygoers to bring a gift. It should be small enough to fit into a shoe box. Agree on the amount of money that should be spent on it beforehand. Each gift should be wrapped by the giver before arriving at the party—and make sure no one tells in advance what they bought.

The host needs to have these items at the party:

 Shoe boxes of the same size (one for each gift)

 Newspaper or tissue paper to pack the boxes firmly

 Wrapping paper, tape, and scissors to wrap the box (you can use newspaper for this, too)

 If you want to get really creative, you can even get some small rocks or paperweights to put inside the boxes that have very small or very light gifts

 A timer or stopwatch

The key here is to make sure that no one can tell what the gift is. As soon as it comes in the door, it goes into a box. The boxes all get taped shut in the same way with the same paper. Mix them up and keep them in another room.

Whoever has the job of putting the gifts in the bags is automatically disqualified from guessing what they are, so you might want to choose a parent for that. No one should be able to pick their gift out of a lineup.

Everyone also needs a notebook or lined paper and pens to write down their answers.

In the telepathy version, each gift is wrapped in disguise as described above, but has a label on it with the name of the person who brought it. This is so that the giver knows what is inside the box but no one else has a clue.

The Rules

THERE are two ways to play this game. One uses straight psychic ability, the other uses telepathy. Before you begin, read the instructions for both versions and pick one. Each version is slightly different, so make sure the gifts are prepared correctly.

PLAY THE GAME: GUESSING GIFTS

The Psychic Version

Get in a circle with the gifts in the center. Whoever was in charge of wrapping the boxes picks out the first gift and puts it in the center of the circle.

All the receivers close their eyes, quiet their minds, and activate their inner senses. Using your clairvoyant, clairaudient, and clairsentient abilities, see, hear, and feel what is inside the box. Write down all the information you receive about it. This is very similar to the Psychic Circle remote viewing game from earlier in this chapter. Set the timer for three to five minutes. After the buzzer goes off, pens down!

Open the gift. When everyone's pen is down, the host opens the gift. Whoever guessed it gets it — simple as that. If more than one person has it right, count the amount of correct statements they wrote about it on their paper.

Everyone guesses their gift during this psychic game. When you give the test this way, everyone will be guessing their gift once during the exam. Honesty is the best policy here. Once the gift is opened, if the person who brought it is the winner, that person should disqualify herself and the second most accurate guess wins instead.

The Telepathy Version

Get in a circle with the gifts in the center. The host picks out the first gift and gives it to the person whose name is on the label.

The gift giver, or sender, holds it in their hands and sends thoughts to the people in the circle. Be as specific as possible. Actively think the name of the gift, its color, size, and shape—you can even concentrate on the activity that is associated with this gift. For example, if it's a small blue makeup bag, you can image putting makeup into the bag, and dumping it out. Set the timer for three to five minutes.

The receivers close their eyes, quiet their minds, and activate their inner senses. Guess what's inside the box. Write down all the information you receive about it. When the buzzer goes off, put the pens down.

Open the gift. When everyone is finished, the sender or host opens the gift. After all the oohs and ahs, screams and giggles, whoever guessed the gift correctly or had the most accurate description of it gets to keep it. Go through all the gifts like this. Whoever has the most developed telepathy wins the most stuff!

Score the Game

SCORING this game is really easy: Whoever walks out the door with their hands full has the most psychic ability. Even if you didn't win a lot of presents, you might still have made some correct predictions along the way. If you want to know your accuracy rate, count up the total predictions you made, along with the ones that were right. Take the number of correct predictions and divide it by the number of total predictions. Multiply that number by 100.

Everyone at the party can do this, and the host can give out runner-up prizes for the highest overall accuracy rates in the group.

Psy-Tips

BY now you know whether you got this or you didn't. If you found it easy, great—just skip this section. If you had a hard time connecting, here are some tips.

First, block out all distraction. You are trying to be psychic in a new environment, under difficult circumstances—and that can be hard. Shut out strange noises, don't think about who is a better psychic than you, don't look to see who is writing what, or who seems to get it. Just relax, bring your attention inside your mind, and get your awareness inside that package.

If you had a hard time picking stuff up, force yourself to write down anything. Begin to draw and see what shapes you end up with. Pretend you are small and you are in the center of the package. Look around and write down what you see. Feel the package against your skin and write down what you feel.

You can even try my favorite trick. Say to yourself, "Okay, I don't see anything, but if I did know what is inside that package, what would I know? Then write it down. Here's another trick: Tell yourself, "In a moment the package will be open. When it is, what will it be?" You can also ask your angels to help you with this.

Practice this at home before your next party. Have a parent or sibling wrap a few things in a few different shoe boxes the way they did at the party. Sit down with the box in front of you, get into a psychic state, and guess what's in there. The more you do this, the better you will become!

Appendix

Dictionary of Psychic
Signs and Symbols

HERE are many common signs and symbols that you'll see as you develop your psychic ability. You may see them as you play psychic games, vision them in dreams, or come across them as you live your everyday life.

If you are looking up a specific item that's not here, find a related object. For example, if you're looking up the word *Apple* and don't find it, look up *Fruit* or *Food*. If your symbol isn't here, do your own inner research. Go back to chapter 2 and watch some Intuition Television or play Revealing Dreams and the subject will come in loud and clear.

If you have a sign that you see often and it has a special meaning to you, go with your meaning over this list unless you are unclear of its message. For example, if your grandmother had a piece of jewelry and you often smile when you see a similar piece on other people, then that jewelry has a different meaning to you than the message in this dictionary.

11:11 Seeing sets of the number 11, especially in this form, means that someone high up on the other side is giving you a message that you are not alone, that everything will be okay, and to remind you that your life is part of a bigger plan. It is a very spiritual and auspicious signal. Also see *Numerology*.

Advertisements If you are seeing the same ad it's no accident. Advertisements in billboards, magazines, and on

TV are a way our sixth sense talks to us. What is the ad trying to tell you? What is on your mind?

Angels Angels are heavenly messengers. They come to reassure us that we are loved and that everything is going to be okay in our lives. If you see an angel, ask it what you need to know.

Animals Animals are messengers, guides, and protectors. According to some new agey studies, everyone has an animal guide. You can discover yours by doing the basic meditation in chapter 1 and asking to meet yours.

Aquarius January 20–February 18; the Water Bearer; rebellious, humanitarian, smart, unemotional. Also see *Astrology*.

Aries March 21–April 19; the Ram; energetic, independent, outgoing, aggressive. Also see *Astrology*.

Astrology The 12 astrological symbols are great indicators of the month of an upcoming event. Seeing the sign name or animal can also signify the different characteristics of that particular sign. Here are the signs, their dates, and main characteristics.

Aries: March 21–April 19; the Ram; energetic, independent, outgoing, aggressive.
Taurus: April 20–May 20; the Bull; secure, loyal, stubborn, patient.

Gemini: May 21–June 20; the Twins; clever, quick-witted, chatty, evasive.

Cancer: June 21–July 22; the Crab; compassionate, sentimental, private, brooding.

Leo: July 23–August 22; the Lion; generous, dramatic, opinionated, attention-craving.

Virgo: August 23–September 22; the Virgin; detail oriented, helpful, organized, nitpicky.

Libra: September 23–October 22; the Scales; charming, sociable, intelligent, lazy.

Scorpio: October 23–November 22; the Scorpion; intense, strong-willed, charismatic, jealous.

Sagittarius: November 22–December 21; the Archer; friendly, philosophical, freedom-loving, unreliable.

Capricorn: December 22–January 19; the Goat; loyal, serious, logical, workaholic.

Aquarius: January 20–February 18; the Water Bearer; rebellious, humanitarian, smart, unemotional.

Pisces: February 19–March 20; the Fish; psychic, emotional, romantic, procrastinating.

Black (the color)   Black is all the colors of the rainbow being absorbed at the same rate. Seeing the color black can mean different things. If you are scared of the dark, black can signify your darkest fears. It can also symbolize the unknown, the dark before the light, something we all experience as we shed our fears and live our lives fully.

Black cat For most people, seeing a black cat means that you are confronting society's fears about something. Remember, they may not be your own but may represent authority or family fears. A black cat can also represent your intuition and deepest sense of knowing.

Blood Even though blood is part of our life force, it is almost never a good sign. It represents pain and fear. If you see blood in a vision, pay attention. Is it yours or it is someone else's? Look to the rest of the vision to determine whether it is a prediction of an event with actual blood or symbolic for an event in which pain and fear are involved.

Blue (the color) The color blue tells you to think calmly and deeply about whatever is on your mind. If you've seen another object on this list and it is blue, it means that the calming energy is influencing that object.

Bottles/containers Bottles can represent things you want to get—whether you have them or not. To determine a specific meaning, look to what they hold and ask yourself some questions. Is it perfume, soda, or shampoo? Is it easy to open or difficult? Is it full or empty? In the vision, do you want it or do you have it?

Cancer June 21–July 22; the Crab; compassionate, sentimental, private, brooding. Also see *Astrology*.

Candle flames (flickering) Candle flames that flicker and make a lot of smoke signify that there is a presence in the room with you, usually an angel, a deceased relative, a spirit guide, or God.

Capricorn   December 22–January 19; the Goat; loyal, serious, logical, workaholic. Also see *Astrology.*

Car   Cars are not only a status symbol, they represent moving toward and away from people, places, and things. Look to the rest of the vision to determine whether you are moving toward or letting go of something and what that thing is.

Charms   When you see a charm or amulet in a vision, it is telling you something about yourself or the person wearing it. Look at what the image is to find out more.

Clock   If you see a specific time in your dream or vision, try to remember it. It is more than likely a prediction of an event that will happen at that time. The number can also have a numerological meaning (see *Numerology*).

Clothing/costumes   Seeing clothing has two meanings. Wearing a piece of clothing, a coat, or uniform that feels uncomfortable means that you are trying to fit in or deal with restricting social pressure. Wearing a beautiful piece of clothing that makes you feel good can mean two things: You are either seeing a part of your soul that you are proud of or envisioning a future goal, something you are very excited about.

Clouds Seeing images of clouds is a reminder of heaven and a brighter day. If the cloud is dark, then there are storms ahead in whatever area of your life you are focused on.

Coins Smile when you see coins in odd places, especially pennies—they are tokens from a higher source to show you that you are on the right track, that you are loved, and that everything will be okay.

Computer/surfing the Net The computer is a great tool for the universe to communicate through. You can talk to your angels and take dictation right into the keyboard. You can also ask a question and see what wisdom pops up as you search the Web. Let your intuitive mind connect the words and images as they come through the page.

Crystals There are many types of crystals, but they are all used to magnify energy to help the user find peace, harmony, love, and success in different areas of their lives. The intelligent glue of the universe uses crystals of different geometric shapes to convey concepts of higher truth and enlightenment. If you are seeing a certain crystal in a vision, this is a sign to find that specific type of crystal and use it in your psychic sessions.

Devil/evil Most often something dark and devilish symbolizes the negative unresolved issues and unconscious fears that you are currently battling or will soon face. Occasionally it can be a prediction about something that will happen to you or someone around you. Often, it's not the event itself that is bad, but how you feel about it. It can appear evil because of something you are unaware of or have a misconception about related to this issue or event.

Doctor Doctors in visions can mean several things. First, they are authority figures who represent our culture, a shadowy version of our parents telling us what to do. Second, a prescription from the doctor in a vision is advice on a deeper level. Third, it's your unconscious's way of telling you that something may be wrong and it's time for a visit to the doctor.

Dog Dogs are a symbol of unconditional love and acceptance. It's easy to see that "dog" is "God" spelled backward. If you see an image of your dog, then take note of the rest of the dream or vision. Was there an additional message?

Doll Visioning a doll represents old familiar beliefs and thoughts or new unfamiliar beliefs and thoughts, depending upon if it is an old doll, a doll you are comfortable with, or a new doll you have never seen before and scares or excites you a bit.

Door or doorway Many psychics see an image of an open or closed door as a sign that they can either go forward with their reading or should stop focusing on that particular question. If you see a closed doorway early on in your development, it may signify a fear you have of the unknown.

Earthquake If the earth is moving during a dream or vision, it means that there is a change in the foundation of your life, a shift in the way you perceive yourself and your world. This is never bad, for it is always followed by growth and renewal, usually better suited to who you are today.

Eclipse In astrology, eclipses separate us from the intuitive energy of the moon or the life force energy of the sun. According to some astrologers, they bring out destructive patterns along their path as they hit the earth. If you see an eclipse in a psychic session, it could mean either that something is being separated from you (temporarily or permanently), or that there is a fundamental change occurring in your life based on some hidden knowledge coming out.

Enemy Seeing an enemy can mean two things. It could be a prediction of something to come with this person, or it could be symbolic for something that you are fighting with, something disharmonious in your own life.

Eye An eye is a gauge or a reminder that something psychic is going on. When one of my clients is psychic, I see the image of an eye.

Falling If you envision yourself falling, your intuition is telling you that something you have or something you want isn't on solid ground. It could also be symbolic of your fears about this subject. Since symbolic images seem unconnected to what they are truly about, you may have to do some inner psychic research to figure out what you are falling over.

Famous person Seeing a celebrity in a dream is common, especially if you were watching TV or a movie right before you went to sleep. Your unconscious uses the characters to send you a message. If you keep coming across images of the same celebrity, ask yourself what that person represents to you and you will know what your sixth sense is telling you about yourself.

Father Seeing a symbol of your father can mean a few things. It can represent society's expectations of you that conflict with your own, or the image can be one of protection and assurance. To determine which one, ask yourself: Does the vision make you feel good or uneasy?

Flowers Flowers represent a positive gift coming, but this gift can come in many forms. You may get an e-mail, phone call, or card from an old flame, ace a test, or learn some good news. Also see *Rose*.

Flying Dreams of flying, or seeing birds or insects, are often a gentle reminder of your feeling restricted in your daily life. When you see birds, something in your unconscious is reminding you of who you are and what you are meant to be. If the dream or image isn't symbolic, it could actually be you flying. Your soul leaves your body when you sleep—where it goes is up to you!

Food Food is nourishing. If you have psychic impressions of food, it means that a nourishing and tasty experience is coming your way. Different foods can signify different types of experiences. To find out what your particular vision has in store, get into a psychic state and explore the food you saw for additional meanings.

Friends Seeing your friends in psychic impressions means a few things. When your intuition is trying to tell you something, it puts familiar people and places together to make its point. To figure out what the vision is actually about, write down all the elements and figure out what's behind them. Also, these images could also be predictions about what is to come.

Fruit Fruit is juicy and sweet. If your intuitive images involve fruit, look at the rest of the vision to determine what sweet and juicy event will happen in your life.

Gemini May 21–June 20; the Twins; clever, quick-witted, chatty, evasive. Also see *Astrology*.

Ghosts/spirits Seeing ghosts can simply mean that your vision is tuned enough to higher vibrations to pick up the energy of other dimensions. If you see a ghost in a dream, it represents an unconscious fear or unre-solved issues that you must embrace and work through.

Green (the color) Green is the color of the heart, good health, healing, and also the color of nature. When you see it attached to an object or person it can only mean good things for them.

Gum Visioning gum means something is stuck to you or you are sticking to something. This can be good or bad—use your ability to decide.

Hearts Your intuition is telling you what is in your heart. Look and see what it is attached to. If the heart is attached to a guy, it's obviously relationship oriented; to get the message, see if the heart is right side up, upside down, or broken. If it is attached to a school or career subject, it is telling you about your career or destiny.

Ice Seeing a big block of ice in a vision means that there is something emotionally, unconsciously frozen that must be recovered for you to truly understand this.

Jewelry Seeing jewelry can mean different things. A ring can mean an invitation or a commitment, and it is another way of saying infinity (since it has no begin-ning, middle, or end). A pendant symbolizes something about you, your hopes and desires. A chain can be something that holds you to a person, place, or event.

Lake A calm and deep body of water represents deep intuitive knowledge and the sense of peace that goes along with that enlightenment. You can either embrace it or be frightened of it, depending upon how you feel about that subject.

Leo July 23–August 22; the Lion; generous, dramatic, opinionated, attention-craving. Also see *Astrology*.

Libra September 23–October 22; the Scales; charming, sociable, intelligent, lazy. Also see *Astrology*.

Lights Many people with developed psychic abilities see lights out of the corners of their eyes or fast-moving lights flashing in front of them. With your sensitive eyes, you are seeing what most people cannot see. This is a normal event and shows you how far you are developing.

Makeup Makeup can make you beautiful, but it can also cover up who you are. When you envisioned it, was it a positive or negative experience? If it felt bad, ask yourself: What is it that you don't want to look at and that you don't want others to see?

Mirror Many psychics stare into a mirror to see visions, guides, and visitors. If you see one in a dream or vision, whatever it is reflecting back at you is telling you something about yourself.

Money Money is a sign of good luck and fortunes ahead.

Month If you keep coming across a date or a month, then something important to you, usually something that has been on your mind, will happen during that month.

Moon The moon represents the mysterious, unconscious emotions. It signifies the emotional stuff going on under your surface.

Mother Seeing a symbol of your mother can mean a few things. It can represent society's wishes for you that are conflicting with your own, or the image can be one of nurturing and unconditional love. To determine which one, ask yourself: Does the vision give you negative feelings or more inspired ones?

Movie Very often our intuition talks to us through things already in our brain. If you have a vision or a dream involving movie scenes, ask yourself what role you are playing and find out what the movie is about.

Numbers Numbers are signposts to events in your life. For example, if you keep seeing the number 3, and you are applying to different schools, that's your psychic ability's way of telling you that you will get into the third school, or one of the first three schools you apply to. For a quick reference to the meanings of numbers, see *Numerology*.

Numerology Besides numbers' personal meanings in your life, they have specific meanings under numerology (the science predicting significant events based on the hidden numbers in your name and birthday). Here are the basic meanings of the primary numbers.

1 — independence, leadership
2 — partnerships, follower
3 — social, always on stage
4 — hard work, craves structure
5 — love of freedom, variety
6 — creates harmony with family and home
7 — observer, secretive, and mysterious
8 — money, power, and business oriented
9 — completion, endings

Orange (the color) Orange is a color of vibrancy, energy, and success. Whenever you see something that is orange, it means the person, place, or event that is connected to it will be successful.

Photos Seeing photos in a dream or vision tells you about the period in your life when that photo was taken. If you keep seeing similar pictures throughout the day, there's a message there. What is in the picture? If you can't determine the message right away, do one of the games in chapter 2 and ask about it.

Pink (the color) Pink is the color of love. If you see pink after you see a picture of someone, that means there is good love potential. Since pink is used to signify a baby girl in Western society, it can tell you the sex of a coming baby.

Pisces February 19–March 20; the Fish; psychic, emotional, romantic, procrastinating. Also see *Astrology*.

Purple (the color) Purple is the color of psychic and spiritual growth. Seeing something purple tells you that you are acting in harmony with your soul.

Rain Rain is very cleansing (except when it floods). If you saw rain in a vision or were rained on in a vision, it means that you or an unresolved issue you have is being healed and cleansed.

Red (the color) Red is a color of energy, passion, and aggression. If something is red, it can be harmless, or it can often signify energy that is too aggressive and threatening. You should take a second look before acting if you have a vision of red.

Relative (deceased) Deceased relatives often visit us in our dreams. You can also feel their presence when you are in a psychic state because your inner senses are activated. If you smell their scent or see their favorite flower as you go about your day, that is a message that they are okay and thinking of you.

Religious symbols or figures Seeing a person or a symbol that has much spiritual meaning to you is a powerful and real experience to remind you of who you are and that you are not alone.

River A moving body of water, like a stream or a river, signifies a flow of energy in your life. If you want to accomplish something, a river is an auspicious vision.

Rose Many psychics and mediums see an image of this flower as meaning one of two things. If you are concentrating on reading someone, a rose is seen as an invitation to go further with the reading. Or it is a visual message from the other side to mean that person loves you.

Sagittarius November 22–December 21; the Archer; friendly, philosophical, freedom-loving, unreliable. Also see *Astrology*.

Scents or smells When you are in a psychic state, you can smell something that doesn't appear to be there. Smelling roses or sweet fragrances is a sign that there are angels or loving deceased relatives around. A sour or rotten smell is a sign that you should not go further with that session.

School Being in a school in your sessions or dreams is your soul's way of learning, and your intuition's way of showing you or teaching you about something. What were you doing or learning when you had that vision?

Scorpio October 23–November 22; the Scorpion; intense, strong-willed, charismatic, jealous. Also see *Astrology*.

Sibling Seeing your sister or brother in a vision means that something is going on with him or her on a deeper level or that something is going on with your relationship with them.

Smoke Seeing images in smoke, or watching smoke move into geometric shapes, is a message from the universe that there is something deeper at work in your life. To find out what, do one of the psychic games in chapter 2 and ask what the smoke is all about.

Spider Spiders don't always have a bad connotation, but because of our culture, more often than not they do. They represent fears creeping up on you. If your vision had a positive feel to it, the spider means unconscious knowledge coming out of the closet.

Sports If your vision involves a sporting event, it means that you are learning, growing, and participating in life. The area of your life is one that you are either focusing on now or will be in the near future. Note the emotions surrounding the vision. Are you excited, scared, or confused? See also *Test*.

Stars If you see stars, you could be remembering your soul actually out and about traveling the universe. If you see a lot of images of stars as you go through your day, your intuition is telling you something about your personal star power or the power of the universe.

Stones/rocks Rocks are earthy and grounding. Native Americans put their worries into palm-size rocks. If you see one during a session, it can be either good or bad. It is either healing or can signify something in your life that is weighing you down or an obstacle in your path. To find out which: How did you feel when you saw that image?

Stuffed animal/teddy bear The meaning of this depends upon whether there is a positive or negative feeling that goes along with this vision. If it is positive, it means a safe and warm environment. If there is fear or negativity, there is something going on behind the cuddly exterior. Beware of what you are not seeing, what is going on inside the situation.

Sun Seeing the sun with your sixth sense is a positive message about you and your goals and accomplishments.

Tattoo Seeing a picture on your skin is a way for your intuition to tell you something about yourself and your unconscious that you may not be aware of. To find out more, look closely at the image.

Taurus April 20–May 20; the Bull; secure, loyal, patient, stubborn. Also see *Astrology*.

Teacher/coach Having a vision of a teacher reminds you of what that teacher taught you, the way they looked at the world, what they expected from you, and how they supported you. This can be either good or bad, depending on whether that teacher had positive or negative beliefs. This symbol can also remind you of your experiences during the time when this person was in your life.

Telephone When you picture a telephone in a vision or a dream or are talking on the phone, someone is communicating a message to you. Ask yourself: Who was on the other end of the phone in your vision?

Television Watching a symbolic television is a good way for your sixth sense to send you a visual message. What images are you seeing?

Test Participating in a test or competition in a dream or vision can mean two things. Your soul is learning and testing itself and its competence. If there is fear attached to the test, you are afraid that you aren't good enough or don't know enough to succeed. If this is the case, decide if you need more time to become comfortable with this area of your life or whether you are ready to go ahead. Don't let your fears stop you.

Thunder and lightning Hearing thunder and/or seeing lightning means that you are about to experience some quick changes in your life or your views about something.

Tree Trees are grounding, healing, and full of wisdom. The tree you see during your psychic sessions is giving you good advice. To know more, ask yourself: What was the subject of this dream or vision?

Underwear Seeing someone's underwear in a vision is seeing their secrets or unconscious desires—the parts of themselves they keep hidden because of their fears.

Virgo August 23–September 22; the Virgin; detail oriented, helpful, organized, nitpicky. Also see *Astrology.*

Wedding If you have a vision of a partnership, it doesn't always mean that you or someone you know is tying the knot. More likely it is a commitment you are making that is life-altering. You may be seeing a wedding, but the subject can involve school, work, a pet—even change of residence.

White (the color)   White is all the colors of the rainbow radiating in balance. It is the color of angels. It signifies that you are acting in harmony with your destiny and your higher self.

X ray   If your vision involves an X ray, it means you are seeing deeply into that situation. Ask yourself, "What do I see?" Sometimes what is happening on the surface conflicts with what is happening on a deeper level. If this is the case, go with your intuition.

Yellow (the color)   The color of the sun is bright, successful, and future seeking. When you see something yellow, it is a symbol of good fortune and luck.

Yoga   Yoga is very supportive to psychic and spiritual growth. Practicing yoga helps activate a deeper level of awareness of the body and mind. If you want to develop your intuition at the fastest rate possible, do yoga twice a week. Within a few weeks you will find it much easier to connect with your deep sense of peace and inner knowing. You will also be psychic for longer periods of time without getting tired.

THANKS TO YOU

I love being able to share my psychic knowledge with others. Every opportunity to write brings me sheer enjoyment—and I appreciate all the people who are part of the process. Once again, I'd like to acknowledge everyone at Warner Books for their support. Thanks to editor extraordinaire Jackie Joiner and marketing whiz Stacey Ashton; also Jean Griffin, Jamie Raab, and Les Pockell. I have great love and respect for my visionary and psychic literary agents Lisa Hagan and Sandra Martin. I would never have gotten this far without them and this is a great place to tell them so! Lastly, I'd like to send a very special thank-you to the most encouraging and loving guy around, Ed Lamadrid.

STACEY WOLF is a professional psychic and spiritual counselor in New York City. She has appeared on numerous TV and radio shows throughout the country. Stacey is the author of *Secrets of the Signs* and *Stacey Wolf's Psychic Living: A Complete Guide to Enhancing Your Life with Universal Energy* and is featured in *The 100 Top Psychics in America.*